Race and Ethnicity in Latin America

Critical Studies on Latin America

Series Editor:
Jenny Pearce
Department of Peace Studies, University of Bradford

Critical Studies on Latin America introduces students and other readers to the major debates amongst scholars attempting to theorise political, social and economic development in Latin America.

Theorizing Social Movements
Joe Foweraker

Surviving in the City
The Urban Informal Sector in Latin America
J.J. Thomas

Race and Ethnicity in Latin America

Peter Wade

Pluto Press
LONDON • CHICAGO, ILLINOIS

First published 1997 by Pluto Press
345 Archway Road, London N6 5AA
and 1436 West Randolph, Chicago, Illinois 60607, USA

British Library Cataloguing in Publication Data
A catalogue record for this book is available from the British Library

ISBN 0 7453 0988 7 hbk

Library of Congress Cataloging in Publication Data
Wade, Peter, 1957
      Race and ethnicity in Latin America / Peter Wade.
          p.   cm. — (Critical studies on Latin America)
      Includes bibliographical references and index.
      ISBN 0-7453-0988-7 (hc)
      1. Ethnicity—Latin America. 2. Ethnology—Latin America-
      -History. 3. Race relations—History. 4. Blacks—Latin America-
      -Ethnic identity. 5. Blacks—Latin America—Relations with Indians.
      6. Indians—Ethnic identity. 7. Latin America—Race relations.
      8. Latin America—Ethnic relations. I. Title. II. Series.
      GN564.L29W33 1997
      305.8'0098—dc21   96-51820
                                                              CIP

Designed, typeset and produced for Pluto Press by
Chase Production Services, Chadlington, OX7 3LN
Printed in Great Britain

CONTENTS

SERIES FOREWORD

This is the third title in the Critical Studies on Latin America series. Previous volumes have dealt with theoretical approaches to the study of social movements in Latin America, and the nature of the urban informal sector. This volume tackles a key theme in the socio-cultural sphere, the changing perspectives on race and ethnicity.

The series introduces the reader to the major debates among scholars attempting to theorise political, social and economic developments in Latin America as it approaches the millennium. The end of the twentieth century is a period of considerable transition in Latin America. The role of the state has been profoundly questioned, yet the more open, market-led economies of the region have not solved the problems of inequality, poverty and poor infrastructure and educational development. Tensions between growth and equity, wealth creation and poverty alleviation continue to overshadow the region, despite its recovery from the economic crisis of the 1980s.

The transition from military regimes to elected civilian governments in the 1980s and 1990s has encouraged some to see an end to the 'pendulum' of Latin America politics in the twentieth century, between 'authoritarian exclusion and populist inclusion'. For some, the research questions now centre on the role of the political parties, changing relationships between legislatures and executives, between municipal and central governments. Others continue to research the persistent social exclusions about gender, class and ethnicity, and their impact on the political sphere, questioning the character and durability of the democratisation processes in the region.

This series aims not to detail the development of Latin America in the social, political and economic sphere, but to outline debates and contested approaches in significant areas. The aim is to enrich our understanding of Latin America at

one of the region's most dynamic periods of development and
to foster discussion on how to conceptualise the processes now
taking place.

Jenny Pearce
Department of Peace Studies
University of Bradford

INTRODUCTION

All over Latin America, and indeed the world, racial and ethnic identities are becoming increasingly significant for minorities and majorities, governments and non-governmental organisations. Once widely predicted to be on the decline, destined to be dissolved by political and economic modernisation, issues connected with race and ethnicity are taking on greater dimensions. Indigenous peoples and the descendants of African slaves – who are the focus of this book – have formed organisations and social movements that call for a variety of reforms to land rights, political rights, cultural autonomy and, in some cases, simply the right to life itself. In some cases, governments have adopted political measures, including constitutional reforms, that recognise the multi-ethnic composition of their nations and accord certain groups special rights, thus moving away from the classic republican nationalism of homogeneous citizenship in which everyone was equal before the state. Such rights, whether given or claimed, are generally in recognition of the historical legacy that these groups are held to have: as original owners of the land, as subjects of enslavement, as the victims of racisms.

In this book, I examine the different ways these issues have been understood over the years. Rather than simply describing the current situation in its many different facets, my aim is to give a critical overview of the debates about the significance of racial and ethnic identities and how to analyse them. To do this, I have taken an historical approach to theoretical perspectives on race and ethnicity in Latin America. On a practical level, I think that current perspectives are much easier to grasp when you know where they are coming from and what they are supposed to supersede. More theoretically, I strongly believe that knowledge is a process that has its own past – an archaeology or genealogy – which it is necessary to know in order to understand its current dynamic. As the metaphor of archaeology or genealogy suggests, present approaches build on, or are generated by, past approaches. It is wrong simply

1

to debunk these as old hat and this is for three distinct reasons. First, while the earlier work done on race and ethnicity sometimes took a line that must be discarded, there were also valuable elements: we cannot now condone the frankly racist view of blacks and native Americans held by some early twentieth-century observers, but the intensive ethnographic fieldwork approach of the 1930s and 1940s set the tone for taking seriously the 'native' point of view in a – not unproblematic – fashion that later approaches would be foolish to deny. Equally, Marxist analyses popular in the 1970s have been subjected to extended critique, but their firm grasp of power inequalities and the importance of an historical analysis cannot be gainsaid.

Second, the perspectives of each period tell us a great deal about that time, about the relations between those studied and those doing the studying, and about the form that knowledge was expected to take. Thus the functionalist studies dominant from the 1930s through the 1950s bespoke a world in which indigenous societies could acceptably be studied as objects located 'in the field' – that is, in some notionally rural area, outside the domain of the anthropologist's urban home society, and also in the field of his (or more rarely her) interest and distancing scientific gaze. Nowadays, the realisation that these indigenous societies are located in and influenced (often negatively) by a broader field of social relations that *includes* the analyst and his or her society makes such an objectifying, scientistic stance much less acceptable. But newer perspectives are built on a critique of the older ideas and the older social order they were lodged in, so an understanding of those ideas and that social order is necessary. A postcolonial perspective makes little sense unless you know what a colonial perspective looked like; the same goes for postmodernist and modernist approaches.

Third, an attempt to understand the present that is uninformed by previous attempts risks not simply reinventing the wheel, but also falling into traps that have been fallen into and resolved in the past. A critical view on one's own perspective is achieved partly by having a good grasp of a range of possible perspectives, including ones that began some time ago.

It is also necessary to locate the academic study of black and indigenous peoples in a wider framework of how these peoples have been seen and understood by their observers, masters, rulers, missionaries and self-proclaimed protectors – not to mention how they have understood themselves. This is a huge area of historical analysis which I cannot encompass here, but it is worth thinking about the continuities between theological ponderings on the nature of the native American in the sixteenth century and anthropological approaches to the same subject five hundred years later. One of the arguments running through this book is that native Americans have from a very early date occupied the institutional position of Other, as essentially different from their observers, whereas the descendants of black Africans have been located much more ambiguously, as both inside and outside the society of their masters and observers. This thread runs through colonial society, appears again in republican Latin American nations and is visible in the anthropological concentration on native Americans to the relative neglect of black people. This reveals that social anthropology, and social science in general, is not a wholly new take on understanding people that emerged in the late nineteenth century; it is part of a longer enterprise of *some* people (typically intellectual Westerners) understanding *other* people (typically colonial and postcolonial subjects, and the peasant and working classes of Western countries). This is another reason for taking an historical view of debates about race and ethnicity in Latin America and it is all the more important when the rights that indigenous and black peoples in Latin America claim and are sometimes given (or have forced upon them) are themselves based on ideas about their historical traditions and status.

The structure of the book is as follows.[1] I start in Chapter 1 by looking at the concepts of race and ethnicity, since a clear grasp of what they mean must precede any further discussion. I then give a broad overview of blacks and indigenous people in Latin America since the conquest, comparing and contrasting their positions in colonial and postcolonial social orders, and in academic study. (It should already be plain by now that my concern is with native Americans and the descendants of Africans, not with the many other possible 'ethnic groups' of Latin America – Jews, Poles, Syrians, Italians, Germans, etc. Any attempt to include these diverse peoples as well would have been to court disaster.) The next two chapters examine theoretical perspectives on race and ethnicity at different periods, from the early twentieth century, through mid-century studies to the more radical approaches of the 1970s. Chapters 5 and 6 analyse in depth more recent developments that locate racial and ethnic identifications within the nation-state and the global context, and that are influenced by postmodernism. The concluding chapter draws the threads together, attempting to find a balance among the different perspectives that have been analysed and reflecting what shape anthropology will be taking in a world which is at once more united by enabling technologies and yet more divided by inequalities of power.

1. THE MEANING OF 'RACE' AND 'ETHNICITY'

Race and ethnicity are not terms that have fixed referents. It is tempting to believe in a progressivist vision of social science that leads from ignorance towards truth – especially with the term race which, in earlier periods, was commonly used in evidently racist ways that are now known to be manifestly wrong. It seems obvious that post-war understandings of the term race are now 'correct'. But I argue that we have to see each term in the context of a history of ideas, of Western institutionalised knowledge (whether social or natural science) and of practices. Race and ethnicity are not terms that refer in some neutral way to a transparent reality of which social science gives us an ever more accurate picture; instead they are terms embedded in academic, popular and political dis- ·courses that are themselves a constitutive part of academic, popular and political relationships and practices.

This does not mean that academic (including social scientific) concepts are completely determined by their social context. Such a rigorously relativist position would be tantamount to abandoning the enterprise of systematic enquiry into our social condition. It would also ignore the fact that such enquiry is, to some extent, driven by the dynamic of its own search after 'truth': when new facts, or new combinations of facts, become increasingly at odds with established ways of thinking about certain sets of facts, this creates a dynamic for change. There are legitimate standards – of logic, coherence, evidence – which mean that not all accounts of 'reality' are equally valid; some are clearly wrong. My point is simply that academic concepts are not independent of their social context, that the search for knowledge is not a steady progress towards a fixed end, but a somewhat contingent journey with no necessary end at all.

This is especially the case with sociological or anthropological knowledge which, however methodologically sophisticated, can never pretend to the rigours of experimental technique that have helped the natural sciences achieve the high levels of prediction and control that underwrite their claims to truth. Part of the reason for this is that knowledge of society is based on people studying people, rather than people studying objects or non-humans, and – whatever the arguments about the level of self-consciousness of non-human animals – this creates a reflexivity, or circular process of cause and effect, whereby the 'objects' of study can and do change their behaviour and ideas according to the conclusions that their observers draw about those behaviours and ideas. Thus social scientists are faced with an ever-moving target which they themselves are partly propelling in an open-ended journey.[1] In this chapter, I want to examine the concepts of race and ethnicity in their historical contexts and argue that we have to see both of them as part of an enterprise of knowledge. This knowledge has been and still is situated within power relations – which, as Michel Foucault has so famously argued, knowledge itself helps to constitute – and in which Western countries have had the upper hand.

Race

Rather than starting with a definition of race which would seem to create a nice objective area of analysis against which previous approaches to the idea might then be judged more or less adequate, I will start with a look at how the term has changed in meaning over time, so that we can see what it has come to mean (without perhaps completely divesting itself of all its previous semantic cargo), rather than what it 'really' means.[2]

Race until 1800

Michael Banton (1987) gives a very useful outline of changing 'racial theories'. The word race entered European languages in the early sixteenth century. Its central meaning was what Banton calls *lineage*, that is a stock of descendants linked to a common ancestor; such a group of people shared a certain ancestry which might give them more or less common qualities. This usage was predominant until roughly 1800. The overall context was a concern with classifying living things and there was discussion and disagreement about why things were different, how permanently they were different and so on. In the concept of race as lineage, the role of appearance was

6

not necessarily fundamental as an identifier. Thus one 1570 English usage referred to 'race and stock of Abraham', meaning all the descendants of Abraham. This included Moses who had two successive wives; one of these was a Midianite (descendant of Midian, a son of Abraham); the other was a black Ethiopian woman. All the sons of Moses by these two women would be of 'his race', whatever their appearance (Banton, 1987: 30).

In general terms, the Bible supplied the framework for thinking about difference: the theory of monogenism was accepted – all humans had a common genesis, being the progeny of Adam and Eve. The main explanations for human difference were environmental and this was seen as affecting both the social and political institutions of human society and bodily difference – often the two were not really seen as separate.

For example, the Swedish botanist Linnaeus (1707–78), whose *System of Nature* was published in 1735, divided up all living things into species and genera, setting the basis for later classifications of difference. He presented various accounts of the internal subdivisions of the genus *Homo*. In one such (Hogden, 1964: 425), 'Americans' were characterised thus: 'Copper-coloured, choleric, erect. Paints self. Regulated by custom'. What we would call cultural and physical features are presented together, showing that they were not necessarily seen as very different, but also showing that what we would now call cultural traits were seen as 'natural': such differences were *naturalised* without being *biologised* (see next section, below).

Banton argues that the use of the term race was quite rare between the sixteenth and eighteenth centuries – the period of the scientific revolution and the Enlightenment – and that ideas about the inferiority of non-European peoples, such as Africans, were not very widespread, especially among the major thinkers of the time. Thus he sees the oft-quoted Edward Long, son of a Jamaican planter, whose *History of Jamaica* (1774) is frequently claimed as showing typically racist attitudes, as an exception rather than the rule. Equally, he argues that Thomas Jefferson, who famously advocated abolition in his *Notes on the State of Virginia* (1787), may have thought of the gulf between blacks and whites in terms of species difference, but was criticised by others for his views.

Banton's concern here is to contest 'presentism', the judging of the ideas of previous historical eras by the standards of our own. This, he argues, tends to lump all these different people together indiscriminately as 'racists', thus losing sight of the complex ways people thought about difference.

This is all very well, but Banton presents us with a history of ideas which is rather divorced from its social context. Audrey Smedley (1993) gives a rather different picture in which the guiding thread of ideas about the supposed *superiority* of Europeans, or whites, runs through the varying and complex ways of conceiving of human difference. The Bible may have implied monogenesis, but it also provided a means for asserting that Africans were inferior. Different peoples were said to be the descendants of the various sons of Noah and Africans were sometimes argued to be the sons of Ham, cursed by Noah for having seen him when he was drunk and naked.[3] In medieval theology, blackness was often linked to the devil and sin, and Africans were often held to be inferior even during the early stages of this period (Jordan, 1977, Pieterse, 1992). Throughout the period Banton refers to, Europeans were generally thought of as more civilised and superior.

Smedley's account – like many others – lays emphasis on the social, economic and political conditions in which the ponderings about human difference took place: explorations of Africa, the conquest of the New World, colonialism, slavery. Following a lead set by Horsman's study of Anglo-Saxons' ideas about fulfilling their 'manifest destiny' of superior political leadership based on freedom and democracy (Horsman, 1981), she focuses on the English and suggests various factors that made them particularly prone to exclusivist ideas of themselves as superior. These factors included the relative isolation of north-eastern European peoples from Greek and Roman knowledge, at least until the Renaissance; the rise from the sixteenth century of capitalism, secularism and possessive individualism (based on ideas of personal autonomy, the importance of property-owning and the accumulation of wealth); the importance given to hierarchy, often defined in economic terms; and the English experience with the sixteenth- and seventeenth-century colonisation of the Irish who had already been relegated to the status of savages (that is, as supposedly bestial, sexually licentious, undisciplined, etc.). This sort of background set the scene for the brutal encounter of the English with the Africans and the native inhabitants of the New World, the usurpation of land as private property and the conversion of Africans into chattels.

Hall (1992b) makes a more general argument about Europe as a whole. He emphasises how the idea of Europe as an entity emerged during this period, from broader and more inclusive concepts of Christendom – which included, for example, black Christian Ethiopians seen as allies in holy wars against Islam (Pieterse

1992: ch. 1). During the fifteenth century, non-European Christians were gradually excluded from the domain of Christendom itself and by the sixteenth century Europe had replaced Jerusalem as the centre of the known world. Despite internal wars and quarrels, Europe was being drawn together by mercantile capitalism and technological development (see also Jones, 1981). It was also being increasingly defined in opposition to Others – Africans, native Americans. The image of the wild man, the savage who reputedly existed on the peripheries of Europe (Taussig, 1987: 212), and of the infidel who had been fighting Christendom for the Holy Land were being increasingly supplemented and displaced by the image of the paganism and savagery located in Africa and the New World – although in all cases, ambivalence (for example, of hate and desire) attached to such images. In short, then, ideas about human difference, while they may have involved a concept of race that was diverse, contested and even not very central, were certainly powerfully structured by ideas of European superiority. Kant (1724–1804), the philosopher whose influence has been so important in Western thought, may not have written much directly about race, but he did comment thus: 'the fellow was quite black from head to foot, a clear proof that what he said was stupid', and David Hume (1711–76) could also state that 'the Negro' was 'naturally inferior to the whites' (Goldberg, 1993: 31–2).

Goldberg (1993) also paints a broad picture. He sees the concept of race as emerging with modernity itself – *'race* is one of the central conceptual inventions of modernity' (1993: 3) – and as intertwined with basic ideas about morality. Whereas in previous eras, morality was defined in terms of virtue and correct behaviour, or of the prevention of sin, in the modern period, and with the Discoveries, people began talking in terms of stocks or breeds of humans people with engrained, *natural* qualities. Human identity and personhood became increasingly defined by a discourse of race, certain races became defined as non-rational or aesthetically inferior (lacking in the 'natural' balance of beauty and harmony) and race could define certain people as fit for slavery.

Race in the nineteenth century

Banton (1987) then moves on to consider the concept of race as *type*. This concept, which built on existing ones and developed in diverse and contested ways during the nineteenth century, was based on the idea that races were permanent, separable types of

9

human beings with innate qualities that were passed on from one generation to the next. Now everyone (or thing) that was alike in nature and appearance was thought to have descended from a common ancestor. Moses' sons, in this view, would not belong to the stock and race of Abraham: some would be considered to belong to the black race, while others might be mixed race, Semites or perhaps Caucasians. Within this overall view, typologies of humankind proliferated and there was heated debate about whether types were separate species or not. Polygenism – the theory that different human types had separate origins – gained ground, despite its divergence from Biblical teachings. Ideas about evolutionary change (in a pre-Darwinian sense), which had been present in the seventeenth century in concepts of the gradual progression from primitive forms of human life (of which the 'lower' peoples were often thought to be exemplars) towards supposedly superior forms, were adapted to ideas about racial types as stages on an evolutionary scale. Racial types were hierarchically ordered, as racial 'lineages' had been before, but now the basis of the hierarchy was thought of in terms of innate differences of 'biology', the term proposed by Lamarck, among others, in 1802 to describe the scientific study of living organisms (Mayr, 1982: 108). 'Natural' differences were increasingly seen as specifically 'biological' differences.

Stocking (1982: ch. 2) compares two French scientists of the early nineteenth century, Degérando and Cuvier. In his writings, Degérando hardly mentioned race and saw difference as environmental, although he did see 'primitive' peoples as being examples of previous stages in progression of humans towards European perfection. Cuvier, sign of things to come, expounded a 'static non-evolutionary tradition of comparative anatomy', and spent his time collecting (or rather stealing) bones and skulls for comparative measurement to assess racial difference. This was an early example of a whole industry of anatomical measurement, designed to specify racial typologies, with great attention being paid to the skull since brain size was held to correlate with superior intelligence. Although many of the practitioners of this science were medics and naturalists, anthropology was often the label they used for their investigations.

This was the age of scientific racism when 'even for self-proclaimed egalitarians, the inferiority of certain races was no more to be contested than the law of gravity to be regarded as immoral' (Barkan, 1992: 2–3). The conceptual centrality which Goldberg asserts for race can also be seen in this statement by

Robert Knox, Scottish medic and author of *The Races of Men* (1850): 'That race is everything, is simply a fact, the most remarkable, the most comprehensive, which philosophy has ever announced. Race is everything: literature, science, art – in a word, civilisation depends on it' (cited in Pieterse, 1992: 49).

The context for the rise of this science – and science it was held to be, even if it was bad science and immoral by today's standards – was the abolition of slavery and the slave trade. There is no easy correlation here, because the apogee of scientific racism was the end of the nineteenth and the beginning of the twentieth centuries, whereas first the slave trade then slavery itself were mostly abolished by 1863.[4] Also, some racial theorists were opposed to slavery on humanitarian grounds, while, conversely, some southern US slave-holders opposed racial typologies on religious grounds (Banton, 1987: 9, 45). But it is no coincidence that just as abolitionist opinion gained dominance in Europe, making the institutionalised inferiority of blacks morally insecure, theories began to emerge that could justify the continued dominance over blacks (not to mention native Americans, Asians and Orientals) in terms of supposedly innate and permanent inferiority and now with the full power of scientific backing. In any case, slavery was partly opposed in terms of its unsuitability for a modern industrial society based on free wage labour (Eltis, 1987), rather than because it oppressed black people, so opposing slavery was no guarantee of a positive stance on racial equality.

The other main social context was the rise of imperialism which, following on from the first main phase of colonialism between about 1450 and 1800 based mainly on settler colonies and mercantile capitalism, began in the nineteenth century to expand rapidly into Asia, Africa and the Pacific with less direct settlement and more emphasis on the extraction and cultivation of raw materials and on the sale of industrial goods. Goldberg continues his analysis of the intertwining of ideas of moral philosophy and racial theory in Western thought by arguing that, in the nineteenth century, utilitarianism became central and that, although the concept of race might not be directly invoked, the principles of utility and the collective good allowed authoritarian rule in which the most rational – the white colonisers – decided on rational grounds what was best for the less rational – the black colonised. Thus John Stuart Mill, the great exponent of utilitarianism, who followed his father into the colonial service in India where 6,000 civil servants controlled vast areas of the subcontinent, preached the need to govern the lower, less civilised orders (1993: 35).

Race in the twentieth century

The twentieth century saw a period of changes and contradictions during which the meanings attached to the term race varied very widely. On the one hand, eugenics emerged as a convergence of science and social policy, the term coined at the turn of the century by Francis Galton, scientist and cousin of Charles Darwin. It was based on scientific racism and the idea that the reproductive capacities of biologically 'unfit' individuals (for example, the insane) and, more generally, the 'inferior races' should be restricted, just as the breeding of domestic livestock might try to eliminate unwanted traits. The movement had quite a strong influence in Europe and the USA and also affected Latin America (Stepan, 1991); by the time it became part of Nazi policy in the 1930s, it had lost much ground elsewhere. On the other hand, however, this period also saw the dismantling of scientific racism.

The latter trend had several sources. Darwin's evolutionary theories indicated that it was no longer possible to think in terms of permanent racial types: breeding populations adapted over time. However, these ideas, published as early as 1871 (*The Descent of Man*) took a long time to impact and did not scotch scientific racism; rather the latter adapted to the former with the development of social evolutionism according to which superior, 'fitter' races were more 'successful' in terms of their capacity to dominate others (Stocking, 1982: ch. 6).

Franz Boas, the anthropologist, also played an important role in challenging scientific racial typologies (Stocking, 1982: ch. 8). A Jew with a background in physics, he left the anti-Semitism of late nineteenth-century Germany and migrated to the US where he did anthropometric research – measuring heads, like many others were doing at the time. He discovered that variation in head dimensions over a lifetime or between contiguous generations exceeded that found between 'races'. The very techniques of scientific racism could be used to undermine its theories. Boas went on to challenge theories of innate racial difference and hierarchy, but it would be wrong to see Boas as the hero single-handedly overthrowing scientific racism. Students of his – such as Ashley Montagu – were also very influential. More broadly, the rediscovery of Mendelian inheritance in 1900 paved the way for

12

the establishment of the science of genetics. Mendel, hitherto a little known Austrian monk, had discovered forty years earlier that specific traits (in sweet peas) were controlled by specific elements (that is, genes) which were passed from one generation to another as independent components; this meant that the idea of 'type', based on a collection of traits passed as an unchanging bundle down the generations, was untenable.

The social context for these changes was varied: imperialism continued apace, legal racial segregation was solidly in place in the US and was gaining ground in South Africa, and the rise of the women's movement and working-class militancy aroused conservative fears of social degeneration which fed into the social reform drive of the eugenics movement. On the face of it, then, there was little reason why scientific racism should be undone. But science had its own dynamic here and the facts that were mounting about inheritance and anthropometry simply no longer fitted into the racial typology paradigm. The racist ideology and atrocities of the Nazi regime in Europe and the upheavals of the Second World War, followed by the black civil rights movement in the US protesting against legal racial segregation, supplied the political drive finally to dismantle scientific racism. This was epitomised in the post-war UNESCO declarations on race which boldly stated that humans were fundamentally the same and that differences of appearance were just that and did not indicate essential differences in, say, intellect.

What happened, then, to the term race in this context? Many biologists, geneticists and physical anthropologists – but not all – have reached the conclusion that, biologically speaking, races do not exist. Genetic variation exists, but it is very difficult to take a given gene or set of genes and draw a line around its distribution in space to define a 'race'; nor can a term such as 'black' or 'white' be pinned down genetically in anything approaching a clear way. Furthermore, most psychologists agree that humans are, on average, the same in terms of their mental capacities; individual variation exists, of course, but there are no significant variations that correlate with categories such as 'black', 'Amerindian', 'white', 'African', 'European' and so on (Lieberman and Reynolds, 1996). Therefore, many natural scientists and the vast majority of social scientists agree that races are *social constructions*. The idea of race is just that – an idea. The notion that races exist with definable physical characteristics and, even more so, that some races are superior to others is the result of particular historical processes which, many would argue, have their roots in the colonisation by European peoples of other areas of the world.

The social constructedness of racial categories can be illustrated by a well-known contrast between North America and Latin America. In the former region, the category 'black' supposedly includes anyone with a known 'drop of black blood'; thus someone known to have had a black grandmother will be assigned a black identity. In Latin America, to over-simplify a complex situation, there is a continuum of racial categories and often only people who look quite African in appearance will be identified as black; people of evidently more mixed ancestry frequently will be classed by a variety of terms denoting a position between black and white. Thus, for example, a Puerto Rican, used to not being classed as black in Puerto Rico, when she moves to the mainland US, may find herself suddenly identified as a black person. The reasons for this contrast are complex, but they are fundamentally historical in nature and connected with the type of colonial enterprise and sets of social relations established in each region. The point is that the term 'black' has no simple referent, even in the Americas: its meaning varies according to context.[5]

Now the notion that races are social constructs does not mean that they are unimportant – 'merely ideas', as it were. Clearly, people may behave *as if* races did exist and, as a result, races do exist as social categories of great tenacity and power. If people discriminate on the basis of their ideas of race, this is a social reality of paramount importance. Equally, people may lay claim to a racial identity that represents for them central aspects of their person – indeed in the US, racial identity is so politicised that no one is really complete without one.[6]

But if races are social constructions, what kind of social constructions are they? Social life is full of social constructions – gender is the one most commonly cited, but ethnicity, as we shall see, is also one, and class could also qualify. Is there something that lets us know when we are dealing with a *racial* construction? Many social scientists argue that races are social constructions built on phenotypical variation, that is, disparities in physical appearance (see Wade, 1993b). The brute fact of physical difference exists and people have used these cues to create ranked social categories which are used to include and exclude and which are said to show more or less innate, natural differences which are passed on over generations: racial identification involves a discourse of naturalisation (Gilroy, 1982; Goldberg, 1993).

This common approach, while it is in my view mostly sound, does however assume that there is such a thing as the brute fact of phenotypical variation. It recognises that races do not exist as objective biological entities, but then tries to reconstruct an objective basis for recognising 'racial' distinctions by grounding them in phenotype. This glosses over the problem that the apparently 'natural fact' of phenotypical variation is itself socially constructed: the physical differences that have become cues for *racial* distinctions are quite particular ones: not just ones that show some recognisable continuity over generations (perhaps height, weight, hair colour, etc.), but ones that corresponded to the geographical encounters of Europeans in their colonial histories. It is specific combinations of skin colour, hair type and facial features that have been worked into racial signifiers.

Thus, to pick up the argument I started with, the concept of race is even more surely linked into a European history of thinking about difference, rather than a concept describing an objective reality that is independent of a social context. To see races as social constructions built on some neutral biological fact of phenotypical variation is to assert that we can recognise a racial categorisation independently of history and build a study of race on an objective basis. In fact, only certain phenotypical variations make racial categories and the ones that count have emerged through history. This means that races, racial categories and racial ideologies are not simply those that elaborate social constructions on the basis of phenotypical variation – or ideas about innate difference – but those that do so using the particular aspects of phenotypical variation that were worked into vital signifiers of difference during European colonial encounters with others (Wade, 1993b).[7] It means that the study of race is *part of* that history, not outside it, and thus that what is to *count* as the study of race is not to be circumscribed by some objective definition about phenotypical variation but can change over time and is, ultimately, up for grabs. This is the only way we can include in the study of race the fact that a group of white US girls triggered an 'imitation race war at their virtually all white high school [in 1994] by dressing "black"'. This had nothing to do with phenotypical variation, but plenty to do with 'race'.[8]

15

Ethnicity

The term ethnicity is at once easier and more difficult: its history is shorter and less morally loaded, but it is also used more vaguely – sometimes as a less emotive term for race. The word ethnicity began in academic parlance and dates from the Second World War (Glazer and Moynihan, 1975: 1; Eriksen, 1993: 3; Banks, 1996: 4), but the word ethnic is older. Based on the Greek word *ethnos*, meaning people or 'nation' (although the latter word has specific connotations since the rise of nationalism in the modern era), it was used in English to refer to heathens or pagans until the nineteenth century, when, with the apogee of scientific racial typologies, it was used as a synonym of racial (R. Williams, 1988: 119). With the dismantling of scientific racism, it began to be used in the phrase 'ethnic group' – for example, by Julian Huxley in *We Europeans* (1936) – to talk about groups that were still seen as biological groupings, without being biological races (Lyons, 1996: 12). Thereafter, the word has generally been employed to refer to groups of people seen as minorities within larger nation-states – Jews or Poles in Brazil, Algerians in France. The proliferating usage of ethnicity and ethnic group, both in academia and in popular parlance, is partly due to rapid processes of social change which have created new postcolonial nations and massive migrations: the terms tribe and race, with which people often used to label the differences that seemed important in these contexts, were deemed inaccurate, demeaning or old-fashioned (Eriksen, 1993: 8–10). Ethnicity has often been used in place of race either because the very use of the word race has been thought to propagate racism by implying that biological races actually exist or because, tainted by its history, it simply 'smelt bad'.

But what does ethnicity mean? Banks collects a useful set of comments from anthropologists and concludes that ethnicity is 'a collection of rather simplistic and obvious statements about boundaries, otherness, goals and achievements, being and identity, descent and classification, that has been constructed as much by the anthropologist as by the subject' (1996: 5). Ethnicity is a social construction that is centrally about identifications of difference and sameness, but the same could be said of race, gender and class – so where does the specificity of ethnicity lie, if anywhere? Some commentators remain vague on this point, but the general consensus is that ethnicity refers to 'cultural' differ-

ences, whereas, as we saw above, race is said to refer to phenotypical differences – although some draw no real distinction
between race and ethnicity (for example, Eriksen, 1993: 5). To
give some substance to this rather bland definition, I will give
some brief examples of how ethnicity has been understood.

Some early influential approaches emerged from the Manchester school of anthropology. Clyde Mitchell, for example, focused
on the so-called Copper Belt mining towns of Northern Rhodesia
(now part of Zambia). People from many different 'tribes' – as
anthropologists then tended to call them – congregated on these
towns and Mitchell observed that 'tribal' identities became more,
rather than less, distinctive in an urban environment through
opposition to each other. People categorised each other in terms
of dress, speech, customs, appearance and so on. Ethnicity – as it
was later to be called – was a way of categorising complex
cultural differences and thus defining for individuals who was
who and how to behave towards them. In the Kalela dance,
urban migrants expressed these differences in a jovial form: as
they danced on rest days in these mining towns, men from each
'tribe' caricatured the cultural traits of other groups and thus
restated ethnic identities (Mitchell, 1956; see also Banks, 1996;
Hannerz, 1980).

Abner Cohen criticised these social classification approaches
and took a line that has since been characterised as an 'instrumentalist' or 'resource mobilisation' model (Banks, 1996: 39;
Williams, 1989). The basic argument was that people used
aspects of culture to signal boundaries and create in-groups
that tried to control some useful resource or political power.
Thus Hausa migrants in the Yoruba town of Ibadan in Nigeria
manipulated aspects of their culture – customs, values, myths,
symbols – to create an ethnically identified in-group that controlled long-distance trade in cattle and kola nuts. For Cohen,
ethnic groups were informal interest groups (Cohen, 1969,
1974). This approach opposed the so-called 'primordialist'
perspective which implied that ethnic identity was just a basic
feature of people's psychological make-up, a product of the way
they classified people, for example. A similar instrumentalist
line was taken in the US by Glazer and Moynihan (1975).

This gives some idea of what ethnicity as discourse of cultural
difference might mean, but it remains rather unspecific: in Britain,
different classes are often thought to have particular cultural features, even if class is principally based on economic differences;
men and women also differentiate each other by reference to

speech, cultural behaviour and so on. In this sense, ethnicity
becomes an unsatisfactory residual analytic category: it includes all
those forms of cultural categorisation where there is no other
primary discourse of differentiation, such as wealth, sex, age,
phenotype, etc.

My own angle on this problem is that ethnicity is, of course,
about cultural differentiation, but that it tends to use a language
of *place* (rather than wealth, sex, or inherited phenotype). Cultural difference is spread over geographical space by virtue of the
fact that social relations become concrete in spatialised form.
This creates a cultural geography, or in Taussig's phrase, a moral
topography (Taussig, 1987: 253; Wade, 1993a: 51). People thus
use location, or rather people's putative origin in certain places,
to talk about difference and sameness. 'Where are you from?' is
thus the 'ethnic question' *par excellence*. Of course, not all objective differences in location are important in terms of people's
perceptions of cultural geography: as Barth (1969) pointed out
many years ago, it is the people involved, not the analyst, who
define what features constitute difference and sameness.

This approach gives us a handle on a commonly noted aspect
of ethnicity, the fact that ethnic identities are 'nested' in a kind
of Russian doll form. Rather than having a single and univocal
ethnic identity, most people have multiple identities according to
with whom they are interacting and in what context. Thus north-
erners and southerners in one country or region may differentiate
themselves (in England, Italy, the US), but identify as the same
vis-à-vis people from a different country (English *versus* Italians),
yet identify with those people in the face of broader differences
(Europeans or 'Westerners' *versus* Africans).[9]

The place perspective also helps to explain why 'ethnicity'
seems to have become a more common phenomenon in the modern world. Although people have doubtless always thought about
difference in terms of place, and although people have migrated
since the origins of the human species, it is reasonable to argue
that with the onset of modernity and a global world – which, for
argument's sake, I will say dates from the late fourteenth century
and the Discoveries – people from different locations in their own
cultural geographies have interacted with increasing intensity. The
rise of nationalism from the late eighteenth century (in the US,
then Latin America and Europe), the later phases of imperialism
(for example, the carve-up of Africa) and postcolonial migrations
(for example, from former colonies to former colonial nations) all
instigated periods of intense re-definition of boundaries and of

social collectivities in which the question of origin in a cultural geography as a defining feature of difference and sameness has become very salient. In this sense, then, as with race, ethnicity and ethnic categorisations are part of a particular history. To see ethnicity as a language of cultural geography is not a final objective definition, but reflects the importance of changing cultural geographies for people in the modern world.

Race and Ethnicity: Is There a Difference?

From the argument so far it may seem that race and ethnicity are distinct concepts. There are, however, two sets of reasons why some people might argue that they are the same. First, some people who do not effectively distinguish between race and ethnicity argue that race should be jettisoned as a term with too much invidious history; they prefer to talk about ethnic relations and ethnic minorities (or, less often, majorities – it is often forgotten that, for example, Anglo-Saxon North Americans are just as 'ethnic' as Italian-Americans). A variant on this view argues that 'ideas of "race" may or may not form part of ethnic ideologies and their presence or absence does not seem to be a decisive factor' (Eriksen, 1993: 5). Anthias and Yuval-Davis do distinguish between race and ethnicity as modes of social categorisation (1992: 2–3), but also see racism as the 'discourse and practice of inferiorizing ethnic groups' (1992: 12). The second set of reasons is more complex and I will argue through it before returning to the first problem.

The dismantling of the biological concept of race and its general acceptance, at least in social sciences, as a social construction has brought about a recognition of the mutability of race – the comparison between North and Latin America discussed earlier is an example. Racial identities are now seen in somewhat the same way as ethnic identities: they are contextual, situational, multivocal. This view is an inevitable result of seeing races as social constructions, which by their nature must depend on shifting social relations, but more recently it also owes a lot to poststructuralist and postmodernist social theories (see Chapter 5). Very briefly, these have led to a critique of a concept of identity as an essential entity, based on the Enlightenment version of the subject as a sovereign, autonomous, rational actor. Freudian theories of the subconscious, Marxist theories of the determination of human consciousness by economic structures, and French structuralist theories of the existence of innate structures of human consciousness which underlie diverse cultural expressions – all these have undermined the Enlightenment view of the subject and led to current views of the subject as fragmented, multiple, unstable and decentred (Hall, 1992a). A corollary of this is an anti-essentialist view of identity: a person, and even less a group or category, does not have an underlying essence or centre that defines overall character (Landry and MacLean, 1993: ch. 7). 'Women' or 'whites' are internally hetero-geneous groups: like subjects, these categories are fragmented and decentred (that is, they have no defining centre). In this view, then, races are like ethnic groups.

It may be objected that racial identifications cannot be as flexible as this sort of view implies: social categories that use physical, bodily cues to assign identities do not seem that open to 'decentring'. There are two issues here. The first is that bodily cues can be used to mean various things: thus a certain skin tone and hair texture in the US might mean 'black', whereas in Latin America it might mean '*mulato*': bodies themselves are socially constructed. In addition, bodies are not immutable: plastic surgery is the most obvious example, but hair-straightening, skin-lightening and sun-tanning are all ways of altering the body that can have an impact on racial identification – and Michael Jackson is only a recent example. The second issue is that anti-essential-ism does not necessarily contest the apparent fixity of racial iden-tifications: rather, the point is that the fact that someone is 'black' or 'white' or 'indigenous' does not therefore say everything about that person. S/he may also be old/young, female/male, homosexual/heterosexual, rich/poor and so on: there are cross-cutting identifications. Thus the point remains that racial identifi-cations seem similar to ethnic identifications: both are partial, unstable, contextual, fragmentary.

My view is that a distinction, based on the approaches to race and ethnicity that I have argued for above, is worth maintaining, although I admit that it cannot be a radical one. The distinction should not be that racial identifications are imposed by a major-ity on a discriminated minority, while ethnic ones are chosen by in-group members for themselves (Banton, 1983: 106). Instead, my point is that to deny a specific role to racial identifications, as Eriksen (1993) does, or to discriminations based on them, as Anthias and Yuval-Davis (1992) do, is to blur the *particular history* by which these identifications come to have the force they do. To identify oneself or others as 'Serb' in Eastern Europe is to invoke a particular, relatively local history; to identify oneself or others as 'black' in much of the Western world is to invoke, distantly or immediately, a long history of colonial encounters, slavery, discrimination, resistance and so on. This does not mean that ethnic histories cannot be long and conflictive, but I think it is necessary to highlight the history of race by calling it by its name.

Neither does this approach mean that racial identifications or racisms are everywhere the same, or that if racism departs from the biologistic version of late nineteenth-century scientific racism it does not really qualify as racism (an implication of some accounts – for example, Smedley (1993), Banton (1987) – that treat scientific racism as a kind of ideal type). There are different racisms, but, in my view, they are linked in historically varied ways to that history of colonial encounters. The meanings attributed even nowadays to 'black' or 'white' in South America, the Caribbean, South Africa, Europe, the US, and also Australia are not independent of each other nor of that history. Racism today in much of Europe, for example, is different from earlier versions in that it depends less on attributions of biological inferiority (although these have not disappeared either). Instead, the so-called new or cultural racism depends on ideas about deeply engrained cultural difference (Barker, 1981; Solomos, 1989; Wetherell and Potter, 1992). Yet many of the current images of blacks, whites, Asians, etc., resonate with previous images.

Racial and ethnic identifications do, however, overlap, both analytically and in practice. At an abstract level, both race and ethnicity involve a discourse about origins and about the transmission of essences across generations. Racial identifications use aspects of phenotype as a cue for categorisation, but these are seen as transmitted intergenerationally – through the 'blood' – so that ancestral origin is important; likewise ethnicity is about origin in a cultural geography in which the culture of a place is absorbed by a person (almost 'into the blood') from previous generations. On a more practical level, if ethnicity invokes location in a cultural geography, it may be the case that the phenotypical traits used in racial discourse are distributed across that geography: in Colombia, for example, 'blacks' are located in certain parts of the country (Wade, 1993a). Also, ethnic identifications may be made within a single racial category and *vice versa*, so that any individual can have both racial and ethnic identities.

Race, Ethnicity and Class

A final theoretical area that needs to be broached is that of the relation between race, ethnicity and class. Here I shall refer mainly to the debates about the relation between race and class, since theoretically this has been the main terrain of dispute and because the issues under debate are basically the same for the case of ethnicity. I will refer to some non-Latin Americanist literature, because much of the debate has occurred outside the context of Latin America and because, in subsequent chapters, I will be looking in detail at race, ethnicity and class in Latin America.

The parameters of this debate are defined by discussions for, against and within Marxism (for more detail, see Anthias and Yuval-Davis, 1992: ch. 3; Gilroy, 1982; Omi and Winant, 1986). The central question is whether race can be 'explained' in terms of class, or more broadly economics. A classic Marxist approach to race argues that the underlying determinant of capitalist societies is the opposition between the owners of capital (the bourgeoisie) and the non-owners (the proletariat); this division, while not fully developed historically, determines much of what happens at all levels in a society. Racial categories must be related to this division and, if they exist, it is because the bourgeoisie has created them in order to (a) better dominate a particular fraction of the work force, who are categorised as naturally inferior and good only for manual work, and (b) divide the workers into antagonistic racial categories and thus rule them more effectively. In these arguments, the origins of racism are located in the class relations of colonialism and the basic functions of racism remain essentially the same over time. This is a simplified version of a classic Marxist argument, but it sets up one extreme in the debate.

Critics of this position may admit that domination of labour and divide-and-rule tactics may be important parts of a racially stratified system and they may admit the colonial origins of racism, but they attack the crude class reductionism of this approach. For a start, it is clear that racial categories can affect economic factors: as we shall see in the next chapter, the fact that Africans became slaves while native Americans were formally exempted from this category was due, among other things, to ideas about Africans and native Americans. Thus the determinations run both ways. Second, the way that racial identifications have changed over time, even in one capitalist country, cannot be easily explained in terms of changing class structures. Thus, changes in racial relations in the US during this century – for example, desegregation – while they may be related to the changing needs of capitalists for a better skilled and more flexible work-force, are also the product of black resistance – as *blacks*, more than as black *workers* – and the dismantling of scientific racism. Third, racism becomes an element of false consciousness, a misapprehension of 'reality': either the bourgeoisie invents it and imposes it on the gullible working class, or the working class somehow invent it for themselves. Neither option really captures the power and 'reality' of racial identifications in daily life. Fourth, class diversity within the oppressed racial category is hard to account for – for example, the position of middle-class blacks.

Over the years, Marxist-oriented writers have shifted positions in a variety of ways to take account of these problems (Solomos, 1986). In broad terms, the tendency has been to attribute more 'autonomy' to racial factors, seeing them as having an impact on economic and class structures and as not reducible to class determinations. Racism is often seen as an ideology which paradoxically, as Anthias and Yuval-Davis (1992: 69–70) point out, actually *determines* the location of racialised groups in the class structure: the Marxist starting point is more or less reversed in that ideology is determinate. John Rex, taking a Weberian approach that is close to some revisionist Marxist positions, argues a similar line (Rex, 1986; Hall, 1980: 314).

Other approaches, not necessarily divorced from Marxist influences, try to avoid the idea that race is 'merely' ideology that intervenes, however autonomously, in class relations. For them race is a level of experience and cultural reality in its own right. Thus, for Gilroy, the struggle of blacks in Britain for civil rights or against police harassment is part of the way the working class is constituted as a political force (Gilroy, 1982: 302). In an echo of Hall's resonant phrase that 'race is the modality in which class is "lived"' (Hall, 1980: 340), Gilroy asserts that the postcolonial economic and social crisis of British society is *'lived* through a sense of "race"' (1993b: 22). Omi and Winant oppose all forms of class reductionism and instead analyse 'racial formations' and 'racial projects' as *sui generis* social phenomena that may be related to class factors, but in which people have their own interests and goals that are defined in terms of racial identifications and meanings (Omi and Winant, 1986; Winant, 1993).

In sum, then, more recent approaches have tended to move away from treating race and class 'as two distinct sets of relations, which interconnect in some essential way' and which are involved in some kind of mutual determination (Anthias and Yuval-Davis, 1992: 75). Rather, and as part of a postmodernist move away from the 'big theories' of social thought – such as Marxism – which try to encompass all phenomena within one totalising and inevitably reductionist explanation, the emphasis is on the multiple ways in which people may identify differences and sameness, struggle, mobilise, and make alliances and enmities. Feminist theory has been an important force in moving in this direction, both in terms of social theory and political action, showing, for example, that black women have different interests from black men, or Asian women from white women (Anthias and Yuval-Davis, 1992: ch. 4; hooks, 1991; Knowles and Mercer, 1992). This has led, particularly in the USA and Europe, but increasingly in Latin America, to debates about the cultural politics of identity and difference which, some claim, distract attention from basic issues of economic inequality (for example, Marable, 1995: ch. 16). In this sense, then, the debate has been reshaped, but has not gone away.

Conclusion

The arguments arrayed above will be important in examining race and ethnicity in Latin America. The differences and similarities between the categories 'black' and 'indian', for example, cannot be understood without a clear idea of what racial and ethnic identifications involve. It has often been argued that black is a racial identification, while indian is an ethnic one. I will be arguing that the difference is not quite so straightforward. Nor can the differences and similarities between Latin America and the US in terms of racial identities and racism be grasped without knowing what these terms mean. Again, it has commonly been said that the US is (or was) the home of 'real' racism, a deep racism based on genetics, while Latin America is characterised by a more superficial racism of appearance or phenotype. I will argue that such an opposition is misleading.

2. BLACKS AND INDIANS IN LATIN AMERICA

The study of blacks and indians[1] in Latin America has, to a great extent, been divided into, on the one hand, studies of slavery, slavery-related issues and 'race relations' and, on the other, studies of indians. Colonial historiography has brought the two together to some extent in synthetic overviews (for example, Lockhart and Schwartz, 1983), but the divide is a deep-seated one. In this chapter, I look at why this divide exists. I argue that the roots of the split go back to the fifteenth century and have spread right through the colonial period, the republican period of nation-building and into the scholarship and politics of the twentieth century. I will also be arguing in this book that such a division is not, ultimately, very helpful and only hides interesting contrasts and similarities between blacks and indians in Latin America.

Africans and Indians in Colonial Latin America

At the time when the Spanish and Portuguese arrived in the New World, Africans were a well-known category of person. Some of this knowledge derived from classical texts, religious sources and travellers' tales; but some of it derived from direct contact with Africa, by virtue of voyages of exploration down the West African coast from the 1430s which had resulted in African slaves entering Lisbon from the 1440s. By 1552, 10 per cent of the population of Lisbon was slave (Saunders, 1982: 55). In addition, the primary experience of the Iberian people (and other Europeans) with Africans was of the Moors, both during the Crusades in the Holy Land and as a result of the Moorish occupation of the Iberian peninsula, from which they were only finally expelled in 1492, after almost 800 years of continuous presence. It is true

25

that Christianity had existed in Ethiopia since the second century and African Christians had fought alongside Europeans in the Holy Wars: in medieval Europe, cults formed around particular Ethiopian figures (Pieterse, 1992: 25). Part of the motive for Portuguese explorations in Africa was the search for the legendary Christian kingdom of Prester John, and Bakongo kings in what is now Angola converted to Christianity as early as 1491. However, because of the long-standing Muslim presence in many areas of Africa – mainly those between the Saharan and sub-Saharan zones – the region as a whole tended to be seen as infidel territory and during the fifteenth century this status was reaffirmed in several papal bulls (Saunders 1982: 37–8).

In contrast, native Americans were a conundrum. There was a good deal of uncertainty about their status, whether they had the use of reason, whether they were real humans, whether they were brutal savages or, alternatively, represented some version of human existence before the Fall (Hulme, 1986; Mason, 1990; Pagden, 1993). Images in colonial discourse are rarely one-sided and with respect to Africans there was ambivalence – infidel or pagan *versus* Christian, slaves *versus* trading partners – but this was particularly evident with respect to native Americans. The dual image of the noble and the ignoble savage that was to flower in the eighteenth century (Meek, 1976) was already captured in the constant representation of indians as cannibals (Mason, 1990) alongside the image of them as innocent beings (Pagden, 1982).

Some of this ambivalence and the difference between Africans and native Americans is evident in the issue of slavery. At the time of European contact with Africans and indians, slavery was considered a normal, if usually temporary, status. There was justification in the Bible and in Aristotelian philosophy for enslavement of the captives of a 'just war' (such as one against infidels), Christians and Moors had enslaved each other, and slaves from the Balkans and the Black Sea area were being used in sugar plantations in Cyprus and Sicily. The conquistadors were keen on enslaving indians in the New World and they received some backing from the regal authorities. Indians could be legitimately enslaved if they were classed as cannibals or Caribs (from which the word cannibal derives) – which in the Caribbean context simply meant those who resisted Spanish rule (Hulme, 1986). One reaction among Spanish thinkers and theologians was to label the indians as 'natural slaves', a category deriving from Aristotelian thought and designating a person incapable of autonomy (Pagden, 1982: 29–30). But there was little agreement on all this and others in the clergy questioned whether a war could ever be 'just' when waged against those who had never known Christianity and who had been defined as vassals of the Crown in Crown territory. The terrible brutality of the conquistadors and the manifest decline of the indian population added strength to these arguments, as did contact with the Aztecs and the Incas whose cities and rule of law were signs of 'rationality'. This was the substance of the famous 1550–51 debates between Bartolomé de las Casas and Juan Ginés de Sepúlveda, but already by 1542 slavery of indians had been outlawed in Spanish colonies. Portugal followed suit in Brazil in 1570. Such legislation was often ineffective in rooting out slavery which continued in many peripheral areas and especially in Brazil where indian slaves fed the north-eastern sugar plantations (Lockhart and Schwartz, 1983: 71–2; Hemming, 1987).

For Africans and their descendants, in contrast, there was little questioning of the propriety of enslavement. There was legal provision for manumission (individual freedom), reflecting the concept of slavery as a temporary condition, and a good number of slaves became free through this means – mostly by self-purchase after years of saving (Bowser, 1972; Klein, 1986). But it was not until slavery as an institution was challenged and dismantled during the early nineteenth century that black people as a category began to be freed in the Americas. During the early period of the slave trade, Africa was infidel territory and the Portuguese had papal authority to wage a 'just war' there; slavery was legitimated as a positive good for infidel Africans; and much of the enslaving was done by Africans themselves, thus masking the question of its legitimacy. Once the slave trade was well under way and the mines and plantations of the colonies so dependent on it, there was little incentive to question such a central institution.

Indians and Africans thus had different locations in the colonial order, both socially and conceptually. Indians were, officially, to be protected as well as exploited; Africans were slaves and, although they had rights enshrined in legislation, this was piecemeal and uneven – although the Spanish did produce a code in 1789 – and the main concern was with control, rather than protection. This difference continued through the colonial period. Ideally, the Spanish would have liked to maintain three separate categories: Spanish, indians and Africans: rulers, tributaries and slaves. Indeed, the authorities talked of the *república de españoles* and the *república de indios*, the latter based on the indian community, created and constrained by legislation. Such an ideal was undermined from the start by the possibility of slave manumission which created the beginnings of a class of free blacks. It was also weakened by the fact that Spaniards' American-born offspring were no longer simply Spaniards, but *criollos* (creoles). In addition, from early on, indians moved into urban areas and Spaniards usurped indian land, while some indians became direct dependents of the developing rural hacienda: both processes weakened the link of the indians to the communities that, in great part, defined their identity as indians (Harris, 1995b: 354–9).

Most of all, the ideal of separation was undermined by *mestizaje*, mixture. The main meaning of this term is sexual mixture, but implied is the spatial mixture of peoples and the interchange of cultural elements, resulting in mixed and new cultural forms. Spaniards, creoles, indians, free blacks and slaves interbred – destitute Spaniards with free black women, indian princesses with aristocratic Spaniards, runaway slaves with indian women, Spanish masters with slave women, free blacks with indians and creoles – and their offspring were recognised as mixed people of various kinds. Racial nomenclature was variable and dozens of labels existed, but *mulato* was the term often used for someone of supposedly black-white mixture, *zambo* for black-indian mixture and *mestizo* for indian-white mixture. Not all mestizos were 'mixed', however, since an indian who disavowed his or her origins could attempt to 'pass' into this category. All these actually or nominally mixed people, in their turn, interbred with others. Some mulattoes were slaves, but most mixed people were free and in many areas they soon outnumbered Spaniards, creoles, indians and slaves (Klein, 1986; Mörner, 1967; Rout, 1976).

Despite this proliferating mixture, the Spanish attempted to maintain categorical distinctions for whites and between indians and the rest. *Indio* was a specific administrative category – in many ways, a fiscal category, since the typical indian was one who lived in an indian community and paid tribute, in labour or goods (Harris, 1995b: 354). It was also a census category, since it was important to enumerate indians as a working and tributary population. In Brazil, where there was less in the way of a dense, sedentary indian population that could be easily exploited through existing systems of political stratification, authorities were less concerned with maintaining strict barriers, but indians still had a specific administrative status. In short, indian was an institutionalised identity.

There was nothing comparable for blacks. The status of slave, of course, was very specifically defined and slave was a central census category. But many blacks were free and they fitted into much vaguer categories which lumped together everyone who was not either white, indian or slave. Thus in New Granada (the basis of today's Colombia), the residual census category was simply *libre* (free person) which included mestizos, *zambos*, freed blacks and mulattoes, and sometimes indians who had evaded their formal indian identity by leaving their communities (Wade, 1986). In Brazil, the middle category was free people which, again, included a broad mixture of people (Alden, 1987: 291). In Cuba (Martinez-Alier, 1989), reference was usually made to *pardos* (literally, light browns), and sometimes also to *morenos* (dark browns). In Mexico, while some local censuses used detailed categories such as mestizo, free mulatto and free black, others simply classed all the racially mixed population as *casta* (Seed, 1982: 577).

This system of socioracial stratification is often termed the *sociedad de castas*, after the term *castas* (breeds, castes) which was applied variously to the middle strata or everyone below the top strata. The term is not used for Brazil and there is evidence that the situation there was more fluid (Mörner, 1967), but the basic situation seems to have been similar (Russell-Wood, 1982: 67–83). In this society, whites were at the top, indians and blacks at the bottom and positions in the middle were defined by various criteria of status, among which colour and descent were very important, without being definitive. Thus occupation could influence one's 'racial' classification in a census, as could the position of one's spouse – although the term 'racial' might not be used, being signified, in Mexico for example, by the term *calidad* or quality (Seed, 1982; McCaa, 1984). People jockeyed for position and trans-Atlantic litigation might take place if someone who claimed to be white felt he had been insulted by being called a mestizo (Jaramillo Uribe, 1968: 181–6).

There has been debate about how open this system was in the Spanish colonies and, in particular, how important 'race' was in defining position within it. Chance (1978) and Mörner (1967) see a relatively open society in which race had a declining role to play as *mestizaje* made racial identifications more indeterminate. Jaramillo Uribe (1968), Carroll (1991) and McCaa (1984) give a greater role to people's ideas about racial ancestry and identity. For Brazil, Russell-Wood (1982: 78) talks of the emergence of a 'meritocracy' during the eighteenth century, but admits that 'the free coloured had to fight to overcome ... discrimination and prejudice', while Lockhart and Schwartz (1983: 403) say that in this period the merchant-planter elite saw the mixed middle strata as a threat in a social order in which 'definitions of social conflict were often perceived in terms of colour rather than economic class'. It would appear that there is no single answer and that a lot depended on local factors, but it seems clear that ambiguity and room for manoeuvre was greatest in the middle ranges: for those at the bottom of the pile, labelled indian and black (or worse, slave), there was less flexibility (Wade 1993a: 9).

The point is that within this system, indians had a relatively institutionalised position, whereas blacks did not: some were in the category of slave, others in that vague middle category of *castas, pardos* or *libres*. It also seems that, although both sets of people suffered great hardship in practical terms, indians were seen in some sense as superior to blacks. This is evident from marriage regulations which allowed whites to marry indians, while restricting unions with blacks and mulattoes. The authorities set out regulations in 1778 which forced whites under 25 years to seek parental approval of their marriage, thus impeding unions thought to be unsuitable. But intermarriage with indians was not restricted, since 'their origin is not vile like that of other *castas*' (Mörner 1967: 39). The Mexican Audiencia, reviewing these regulations, commented on marriage between indians and blacks or mulattoes, recommending that parish priests be ordered to warn the indian and his parents of the serious harm that 'such unions will cause to themselves and their families and villages, besides making the descendants incapable of obtaining municipal positions of honour in which only pure Indians are allowed to serve' (cited in Mörner 1967: 39).

In sum, then, indians and blacks had different relationships to the official structures of bureaucracy. Since the relationship between law and social order is notoriously difficult to establish, it would be dangerous to argue that this difference translated directly into an identical difference in popular colonial perceptions of blacks and indians, or in conditions of material welfare. Indeed, indians were often treated extremely badly. But the laws themselves, especially those of the late colonial period, were in part a reflection of white elite concerns and it is clear that the category indian, for example, was not simply a legal fiction, but an everyday reality, reconstituted through daily practice.

Blacks and Indians in the New Republics

With independence, the former Spanish colonies began to dismantle the administrative trappings of empire, although Brazil gained

30

independence as an empire in its own right until it became a republic in 1891, while Puerto Rico and Cuba remained colonies of Spain
until 1898. Under the pervasive influence of European liberalism,
the status of indian and, more particularly, indian land came under
attack. There were widespread moves to disestablish indian communities and undermine the existence of a separate category of
people who had a legal position distinct from that of simple citizen.
These were frequently ineffective and in the Andes 'there were
strong local vested interests in maintaining a distinctive category of
Indians' (Harris, 1995b: 363). Legal discriminations against mixed
bloods were gradually removed and by 1854 slavery was abolished
in the new republics; it was retained in Brazil until 1888, in Puerto
Rico until 1873 and in Cuba until 1886 (Bauer, 1984; Grieshaber,
1979; Halperín Donghi, 1987). However, ideas about race and
about categories of people called indians, blacks or mestizos were
by no means removed from the national panorama. Again, there
was a distinct difference between the images of blacks and indians
in debates about the identity of the new nations – or empire in the
case of Brazil.

Ideas about race were crucial elements in discussions about
national identity in a world where European and North American
nationalisms already dominated the stage. Latin American elites
wanted to emulate the modernity and progress of these nations
and accepted in broad terms the tenets of liberalism which saw in
science, technology, reason, education and freedom of the
individual the underlying forces of progress. But these modern
and progressive nations either had no significant black or indian
populations, or, in the case of the US, kept them strictly segre-
gated. In contrast, most Latin American countries had substantial
numbers of mestizos, blacks and indians. Worse still, by the late
nineteenth century, the theories of human biology accepted in
Western scientific racism relegated blacks and indians to a
permanently inferior status and condemned mixed-bloods as
degenerate.

Latin American elites tried to deal with this contradiction by
adapting Western theories of human difference and heredity. The
racial determinism of European theories was often avoided and
emphasis placed instead on the possibility of improving the population through programmes of 'social hygiene', improving health
and living conditions. Lamarckian theories about the heredit-
ability of characteristics acquired during a single lifetime were
popular, since these held out the hope of lasting improvement of
'the race' (Stepan, 1991). The idea of the degeneracy of the

31

mestizo was contested, and indeed in nations such as Colombia
or Mexico mixedness became a symbol of a distinctive Latin
American identity, free from the slavish emulation of European
or North American masters.

On the other hand, the type of mixedness invoked was often
itself biased towards whiteness: European immigration was often
encouraged or even sponsored by the state, and more generally,
the process of mixing could be seen as a progressive *whitening* of
the population. Mixture would supposedly bring about the elimi-
nation of blacks and indians and the creation of a mixed society
that was at the distinctly whiter end of the spectrum. Such a
vision was almost magical, since every instance of race mixture
must logically be a darkening as well as a whitening, but the
vision was sustained, on the one hand, by eugenic notions that
white 'blood' was stronger than other types and would naturally
dominate in the mixture and, on the other, by immigration policies which tried to restrict the entry of blacks. These ideas and
processes were common, in varying ways, to Brazil, Venezuela,
Cuba, Argentina and Colombia, among others (see Graham,
1990; Helg, 1995; Skidmore, 1974; Stepan, 1991; Wade, 1993a;
Wright, 1990).

In the attempt to delineate a distinctive national identity, reference could be made (or could not be avoided) to the historical
roots of the nation. From the 1920s, the indian became a prime
symbol of national identity in countries such as Mexico and Peru:
both countries created government departments for indigenous
affairs, while Peru recognised the 'indigenous community' as a
legal entity and Mexico created academic institutes dedicated to
the study of indigenous peoples. In Brazil, an agency was set up
in 1910 for the 'protection of the indians'. This, in broad terms,
was the ideology of *indigenismo*. This term covers a variety of
perspectives, but the central notion was that indians needed
special recognition and that special values attached to them. Very
often, it was a question of exotic and romantic symbolism, based
more on the glorification of the pre-Columbian indian ancestry of
the nation than on respect for contemporary indian populations.
Thus the reality was often one of continued discrimination and
exploitation. In addition, the future was generally envisaged as
being integrated and mestizo in colour.

Manuel Gamio, for example, who became director of the
Instituto Indígena Interamericano in Mexico, undertook archaeo-
logical investigations of Teotihuacán and also began studies of
contemporary indian communities. At the same time, his overall

perspective was integrationist and conformed to the typical ideas of nation-building based on education and incorporation (Brading, 1988; Hewitt de Alcántara, 1984: 10). For Mexico, 'post-revolutionary *indigenismo* ... represented yet another non-Indian formulation of the "Indian problem"; it was another white/mestizo construct ... part of a long tradition stretching back to the Conquest' (Knight, 1990: 77). In Brazil, as well, 'every indigenist project aimed to solve the problem of transforming the Indian from ... "savagery" to the superior stage of "civilization"' (Lima, 1991: 246). On the other hand, some *indigenistas* adopted much less integrationist positions. Peruvians José Carlos Mariátegui (1895–1930) and Víctor Raúl Haya de la Torre, for example, took a more radical line, wedding socialism and *indigenismo* and modelling the future nation on the supposedly socialist aspects of ancient Andean indian culture (Hale, 1984; Chevalier, 1970). Such a view responded in part to the fact that a dense indian population still lived in the Andes. Whatever the variety, however, the point remains that indians were often seen as a special category, needy of the specific attention of intellectuals, the state and the Church.

Blacks were much less likely to be symbolised in this way and were rarely held up as the symbols of a glorious heritage. Only in Cuba and Brazil, with their very large black populations, was there a positive revaluation of blackness in some quarters, although, again, this tended to be integrationist in tone, with the emphasis on the emergence of a mixed society in which a black input was valued as long as it was under control. Even then, the trend was mainly literary, with little discernible impact on government policy.

In Cuba during the 1920s and 1930s, there was a trend of *afro-cubanismo* in literary circles with authors such as Alejo Carpentier and Nicolás Guillén leading the way (Bueno, 1993; McGarrity and Cárdenas, 1995: 92; Prescott, 1985). Franco (1967: 103–32) argues that this was inspired by the European avant-garde view of primitivism as an alternative to scientific rationality. Afro-Cuban music was also making an impact within the country and internationally (Manuel, 1995; Roberts, 1979). Even though there were strong elements in these trends of the appropriation by whites of exotic aspects of black culture – blacks were an infrequent sight in the dance orchestras that played Afro-Cuban music (Díaz Ayala, 1981: 158) – it was nevertheless a departure from the image of blacks as simply backward and inferior.

In Brazil, musicologist Mário de Andrade also accepted

African musical elements as a valuable part of a mixed Brazilian national music (Reily, 1994), but it was Gilberto Freyre who really attempted to produce a vision of Brazil that went beyond the dilemmas created by scientific racism which had branded the country as racially hybrid and therefore inferior (Skidmore, 1974: 184–92). Policies of whitening through immigration still existed, but by Freyre's time scientific racism was on the wane – in any case some Brazilian thinkers had tried to avoid the most determinist versions of it. Freyre's aim was to redefine the Brazilian nation as mixed – and proud of it. Even so, his view was highly assimilationist. In his book, *Brazil: An Interpretation* (1951), for example, he stated:

> Brazil stands today as a community from whose experiment in miscegenation other communities may profit. Probably in no other complex modern community are problems of race relations being solved in a more democratic or Christian way than in Portuguese America. And Brazil's experiment does not indicate that miscegenation leads to degeneration. (pp. 98–9)

This declared Brazil to have actually benefited from race mixture, since this had solved problems of race relations. He also said that Brazilians generally feel that 'nothing is sincerely or honestly Brazilian that denies or hides the influence of the Amerindian and the Negro': *authentic* Brazilian identity was therefore mixed (p. 122). On the other hand, he declared: 'Negroes are now rapidly disappearing in Brazil, merging into the white stock' (p. 96) and although 'Brazil still has to face the problem of assimilating certain Amerindian tribes as well as those groups of Negroes whose culture remains largely African', this was not a major problem since 'the general tendency among broad-minded Brazilians [he admits that not all of them are] is to maintain, towards Africans as well as Indians, a policy of slow and intelligent assimilation, in which the assimilating group may incorporate into its culture certain values of general interest or artistic importance' (p. 119).

Some of this – not all – was very optimistic, indeed naive, stuff when applied to the realities of Brazilian social structure and culture, but it was an attempt to redefine Brazilian identity as something other than a slavish copy of Euro-American nations and yet still 'complex [and] modern'; it is, in effect, a redefinition of modernity away from whiteness towards hybridity – a move that prefigures more postmodern discussions that also welcome

Latin America's hybrid nature (García Canclini, 1989; Schwarz, 1992: 1–18).

The central point, however, is that the sort of redefinition of national identity attempted by some Cuban and Brazilian intellectuals and scholars was, in the Latin American context, limited in the way it dealt with blacks, as compared to indians. Most important, perhaps, these attempts were at the level of image, representation and literary and musical productions; they rarely involved state policy. *Indigenista* approaches generally did involve policy, thus continuing the tradition of reifying indians as an object of official attention.

Blacks and Indians in Politics and Social Science

The different location of blacks and indians in the political and imagined space of the nation has not received much attention from scholars, but it seems to me of great importance: it has had significant political consequences and has also affected the way each category has become an object of study in academia. Colombia is a good example of this difference and its consequences.

Indians in Colombia have suffered terrible discrimination and abuse and still suffer today. Yet legally and conceptually they have a special position. Legislation in 1890 reaffirmed the existence of indian *resguardos* (reserves) and indian councils to govern them. In 1941, the state created an institute of ethnology whose main purpose was to study indian society and history. Since the beginnings of its academic institutionalisation in the country in the 1940s, most anthropological work has focused on indians. The premier Gold Museum in Bogotá focuses exclusively on pre-Columbian indians, even though there were important gold-working traditions in the regions of Africa whence came a good part of the population of the country. Indian mobilisation to fight for land and rights has been a significant force since the 1960s and important concessions – on paper at least – have been won. Legally, indians who form about 2 per cent of the nation's population now own about 22 per cent of its territory in the form of reserves – although practical enforcement of that ownership is a different matter. In the 1991 constitutional reform, indian groups won important rights, including the right to two seats in the Senate (Arocha, 1992; Jackson, 1995; Wade, 1993a: 352–5, 1995a).

Blacks, in contrast, have according to Friedemann (1984) been made 'invisible' in the nation – systematically ignored, marginalised and belittled. I would argue that things are not quite so straightforward, in the sense that commentators on Colombian national identity have, for over a hundred years, always recognised the existence of blacks, but it is true that this has often only been to disparage them or caricature them in some way. It is certainly true that academically they have hardly been studied – not constituting the cultural Otherness that anthropology has sought among indians – and that politically they have simply been seen as ordinary citizens, even while in practice they suffer racial discrimination (Wade 1993a). Black political mobilisation has been much weaker than that of indians and in the 1991 constitutional reform, black groups fared much worse in terms of extracting concessions on land rights and cultural recognition – although in both respects they did make ground-breaking steps in the direction of being constituted as a specific cultural, political and conceptual category within the nation (Wade, 1995a; Arocha, 1992; Friedemann and Arocha, 1995).

This contrast, in my view, has its roots in the history I have outlined above and the result in academic terms has been the general separation of studies of blacks from those of indians – with some notable exceptions such as Whitten (1981a) and Taussig (1980, 1987) – and the relative neglect of blacks – with the main exception of Brazil where, even so, indians have been the domain of anthropology, while blacks have generally been studied by sociologists. In the face of this, one tendency is to focus on blacks, bemoaning their neglect in academic circles compared to studies of indians and seeking to redress it: this highlights the differences between 'black' and 'indian' as categories. Another tendency is to see blacks and indians as rather similar: both are seen as minorities in nation-states intent on a future of homogeneity; both are at the bottom of a ladder which represented parallel hierarchies of wealth, education, civilisation and race; both are inputs into the progressive, modernising process of whitening the nation (Stutzman, 1981; Whitten, 1985; Wade, 1993a).

Neither perspective is wholly right or wrong. The point is to bring blacks and indians into the same overall theoretical perspective, especially in the context of the Latin American nation, while also recognising the historical, political and conceptual differences that do exist between these categories. Blacks and indians have both been characterised as Others, located in the liminal spaces of the nation, but they have fitted in different ways into what I call the structures of alterity. The apparent 'invisibility' of black people in Colombia, for example, has not been due to a simple process of discrimination – indians have, if anything, suffered even greater discrimination – but due to the precise mode of their insertion into the structures of alterity. They have not been institutionalised as Others in the same way that indians have. Interestingly, however, there has been a relatively recent appearance of blacks on the public political stage in Colombia, Brazil and Nicaragua where constitutional measures recognise the special status of blacks in general or particular groups of blacks (see Chapter 6). In some sense, this corresponds to a relocation of 'blackness' in structures of alterity in ways that make it look increasingly like 'indianness'.

Blacks and Indians, Race and Ethnicity

Another way that the split between blacks and indians has been introduced into social science is with the virtually unquestioned assumption that the study of blacks is one of racism and race relations, while the study of indians is that of ethnicity and ethnic groups. The principal idea underlying this is that the category 'indian' does not depend on phenotypical signifiers. As I mentioned above, during the colonial period, the identity 'indian' depended partly on being located in an indian community; leaving that community, which might also involve leaving aside typically 'indian' clothing and language, was a step on the path to becoming a 'mestizo'. Studies in the twentieth century have reinforced this: 'indian' is a category defined by cultural signifiers (clothing, language, place of residence, etc.) and the boundary between indian and mestizo is potentially crossable by manipulating those signifiers (Bourricaud, 1975; Harris, 1995b; van den Berghe, 1974a: 15). In contrast, 'black' is often seen as a category defined by more fixed phenotypical criteria that cannot be manipulated in the same way.

There are two sets of problems here. The first is that it is wrong, in my view, to see indians simply as an ethnic group or set of ethnic groups. The category 'indian' was an integral part of the colonial encounters within which the discourse of race emerged and, for example, the debates about the fate of the nation that took place in Colombia in the late nineteenth and early twentieth centuries talked in similar terms about the supposed failings of 'indian blood' and 'black blood'. From a macrohistorical perspective, then, 'indian' was a racial category and retains strong elements of this history.[2]

The other set of problems relates to the microscale. There is no doubt that, on an individual level, 'indians' can become 'mestizos'; it is also true, however, that 'blacks' can become 'mulattoes'. As I argued in the previous chapter, it is mistaken to assume that, just because racial signifiers are bodily, they are completely fixed. Part of this assumption comes from the classic US case where racial identification has been very rigid and an attempt has been made to create very tightly bounded categories of black and white. Even there, 'passing' occurs, so that an individual who is classed as black in some circumstances 'passes' for white in others; and blacks may also lighten their skin and straighten their hair. Spike Lee in his film, *Jungle Fever*, cleverly plays with US racial identifications by introducing a dark-skinned character who seems at first to be African-American, but turns out, from his speech, to be Italian-American – and rabidly anti-black. The main point is that it is wrong to extrapolate from the US case to racial identifications in general. The Latin American material shows that, for example, the same individual dressed shabbily and smartly will be identified with different colour terms that locate the person on a scale between black and white. These terms are not dependent on phenotype alone, because the context of somatic features alters people's classification – and even perhaps perception – of these features (Solaún and Kronus, 1973). It is also widely reported that 'the blacks' is often a term used more or less synonymously with 'the poor' (for example, Harris, 1952), indicating again that economic status influences racial classifications. Thus identifications of 'black' are malleable, as well as those of 'indian'.

It is also worth bearing in mind, however, that such malleability is not complete. The indian migrant from the highlands of Peru who becomes a domestic maid in Lima is on her way to becoming a mestizo woman, but her background is not forgotten; the term *cholo* is frequently used to identify people who are seen as 'between' indians and mestizos (Radcliffe, 1990). Equally, people who, by local standards, have *typically* indian or black somatic features have a hard job losing that identity, even if they are not publicly labelled as indian or black (Watanabe, 1995: 31). In Latin America, people are generally quite sensitive to the possibilities of ancestry that can be inferred from appearance, so such signifiers cannot be erased completely by changing other cues.

This is not to argue that the categories of black and indian are therefore exactly the same in terms of the processes of identification they involve. Each category has a different history with different possibilities and modes of construction and transformation, modes that also depend on local contexts. The use of 'race' to talk about black identity and 'ethnicity' to talk about indian identity is fair enough *as long as* it is recognised that the difference between them is not one of *opposition* between racial and ethnic classifications. Such an opposition separates phenotype from culture, as if the former was not itself culturally constructed. Both 'indian' and 'black' are, in my view, categories that have aspects of racial and ethnic categorisation.

In sum, then, I think it is necessary to bring blacks and indians into the same theoretical frame of reference, while recognising the historical differences between them and the consequences of these at a political level. However, as the succeeding chapters will show, blacks and indians have generally been dealt with separately.

3. EARLY APPROACHES TO BLACKS AND INDIANS, 1920s–1960s

Indians: Integration and Isolation

There were essentially two overlapping contexts for thinking about and studying indians in Latin America before the Second World War. On the one hand, there was the 'problem' of indians in the national frame with which *indigenista* thought in all its varieties was concerned. This was a theme debated by intellectuals and politicians and policy was always a central issue since the 'problem' was that of how (or sometimes whether) to integrate indians into the modernising nation.

The other context was that of international social science, shaped by the North American and European academies. This was never disconnected from the first context and indeed increasingly integrated with it, in the sense that some of the Latin Americans concerned with policy issues of (non-)integration in their countries were themselves trained in Euro-American social science – after all, a School of American Archaeology and Ethnography was founded in Mexico by German-American Franz Boas as early as 1909. However, although policy was not irrelevant in this context, it tended to take a back seat to 'scientific' study. Here functionalism was an important theoretical perspective from about the 1930s up to at least the 1960s. In anthropology, this approach tended to focus on particular (non-Western) communities with the aim of discovering their internal mechanisms of social integration. The method was intensely ethnographic, based on living in the community for a long period and preferably learning the local language, and issues of social change and national context tended to be sidelined in favour of studying structural and cultural patterns within the community. Also influential in the academic context was North American cultural ecology which, beginning in the 1940s attempted to see cultural patterns and social structure as ecological adaptations. Finally, French structuralism was important for many anthropologists and was pioneered in the Latin American context by Claude Lévi-Strauss who first did fieldwork in Brazil in the 1930s; the full impact of this theoretical approach was not felt, however, until the 1960s.

Geographically, there were three main areas of study: the Andes, Mesoamerica (particularly Mexico) and Amazonia. In the latter area, although *indigenismo* was an internal policy issue in Brazil from at least 1910 (Lima, 1991), questions of racial and ethnic identities and relations were not broached in an academic context until late in the period under review and, when they were, the concern was mainly with indians as victims of genocide. Initially, then, the first two areas will be my principal focus.

Mallon notes a difference between Mexico – where the forces and ideology of *mestizaje* took precedence, defining mestizos as central and indians as peripheral – and the Andes where the indian population was much larger and there were more 'bi-polar' constructions based around images of the indian highlands and plateaus and the white/mestizo coast and valleys (Mallon, 1992: 35–8). Nevertheless, common to both areas was a basic conceptual division between indians and mestizos. Thus in Mexico, the rural mestizos were seen as peasants and class was the central analytic category for historians and anthropologists; in contrast, indians lived in peripheral regions and could be studied in their own terms. Similarly in Peru, indians were seen as 'traditional', gradually being incorporated into the modern market economy which was the domain of mestizos and thus becoming mestizos themselves, perhaps via the intermediate category of 'cholo' (Mallon, 1992). In general, then, class was associated with mestizos and, although the word was not necessarily used, ethnicity with indians. At the same time as an overall modernisationist perspective implied that class would eventually erase ethnicity and although *indigenistas* were concerned with problems of integration into national society, or the lack of it, there was a sense that indians could be studied as isolated groups and communities.

Another common feature uniting Mesoamerica and the Andes was the difference between the so-called closed corporate indian communities and the more open integrated communities. The distinction was initially made for Mesoamerica where the closed communities were those that had attempted to maintain a certain defensive isolation – for example in central and southern Mexico (including Chiapas) and in highland Guatemala, (Nash, 1970; Wolf 1955). The contrast was with more open communities, often in more lowland areas, that had historically been more integrated and their 'indian' identity correspondingly weaker. The same distinction was later made for Peru, contrasting the highlands to the coastal regions (Grieshaber, 1974a: 120).

Functionalist approaches in Mexico

In Mexico, studies of indians in the 1930s and 1940s were mainly in the classic functionalist mode. On the one hand, *indigenistas* such as Manuel Gamio were interested in researching pre-Columbian indian history and in studying contemporary indians in order the better to 'improve' their lifestyle and integrate them. As part of this trend, Mexicans and some early North American anthropologists were carrying out ethnographic studies of the ways of life of the indians who seemed the most 'traditional' and un-touched. On the other hand, US anthropologists such as Robert Redfield began in the 1920s the functionalist study of so-called 'folk' communities – ones that were indian, but were also far from untouched, having had a long experience of interaction with non-indian people (as, in reality, had even the most apparently isolated communities). His footsteps were accompanied and followed by important scholars, including Ralph Beals, Oscar Lewis and George Foster. In the 1950s, the Harvard Chiapas Project sent scores of anthropologists, graduate students and professionals – including Evon Vogt and Francesca and Frank Cancian – to the Chiapas region of southeastern Mexico to do community studies which were often still highly functionalist in approach, despite the mounting critiques directed at this approach for its assumptions of integration and harmony, and its neglect of history, conflict and the wider context (see Hewitt de Alcántara, 1984: chs. 1 and 2, for a discussion of this period).

These anthropologists differed widely amongst themselves – for example, Lewis (1951) re-studied Tepoztlán, the subject of an early book by Redfield (1930), and found envy and dissent instead of harmony and cooperation – but with regard to ethnic or race relations, many of them had rather little to say. Redfield dealt tangentially with the issue by means of his folk–urban continuum which posited an ideal-typical traditional pole of the almost untouched community at one end, going through the folk community and the local town, to the regional city at the other end. Along the continuum, people's values and social relations gradually became more 'modern' (by which he meant more individualistic, more secular, less homogeneous and more governed by class structures and the market). Change, or 'acculturation', occurred through contact of more traditional with more modern ways. Apart from the obvious flaws of such a one-way dynamic, based more on the decontextualised exchange of attitudes than on economic and political relations, there is little here that tells us about ethnic and racial identifications. On the contrary, the implication was that the difference between 'indian' and 'mestizo' could be measured on a linear scale of the presence or absence of objective traits and attitudes: this hardly captures the complex processes of contextual identification of self and other that lie at the heart of identity.

More direct treatments of ethnic relations did, however exist in the functionalist mould. Sol Tax (1942), Melvin Tumin (1952) and John Gillin (1951) wrote on the topic in relation to Guatemala, as did Redfield himself at a later date (Redfield, 1956). Gillin and Tumin argued that indians and mestizos (or ladinos as they were called there) had relations of 'caste' – that is, two very separate groups were divided by a strong social barrier similar to the black–white boundary of the US at the time – and there was a good deal of argument about the appropriateness of this term to cover a variety of local contexts (see Aguirre Beltrán, 1979: ch. 8). Mexico, for example, was often seen as being more fluid.

Despite this usage, the functionalist approach to interethnic relations tended to emphasise harmony and interdependence rather than conflict and exploitation. As Hewitt de Alcántara notes (1984: 64–6), scholars such as Sol Tax and Manning Nash made use of concepts of pluralism, originally derived from the work of J.S. Furnivall on Burma. Pluralism tried to account for the continued existence of different cultural groups in a single society in terms of their common participation in certain institutions, especially economic and political ones; this was what created underlying social integration. Although later versions of pluralism emphasised the existence of coercion in this situation, 'members of the Tax-Nash school supposed that Indians and non-Indians interacted principally because they needed each other and received a necessary service during the exchange' (Hewitt de Alcántara, 1984: 66). That is, a benign and harmonious interdependence and complementarity underlay ethnic relations. Indians were poor because they were isolated and had yet to acquire the knowledge, skills and technology for a more prosperous life. Economic development should be planned so as to allow this, without imposing total cultural assimilation.

One common corollary of these functionalist and pluralist approaches was the idea that indian culture was traditional and thus a brake on the process of modernisation that was widely assumed to be occurring or at least desirable. The classic formulation of this view was actually developed in relation to peasants rather than indians and is found in George Foster's notion of 'limited good' based on his work in the mestizo village of Tzintzuntzan from 1948 onwards (Foster, 1967). According to Foster, peasants thought that the sum total of value available to them all was limited; thus anyone who became richer was doing so at the expense of others; this generated intense envy, conflict and distrust and these psychological dispositions inhibited expansion and growth. This world view was the result of centuries of colonial domination, but had crystallised into a self-perpetuating attitude. Critics of Foster pointed out that his argument tended to blame the poor for being poor, that their poverty depended much more on external circumstances than their psychological attitudes and that, if opportunities for growth were presented in the appropriate form, 'traditional' peasants would take advantage of them (Long, 1977: ch. 3).

Reading between the lines of this body of work, one finds the underlying premise – typical of a community-level functionalist approach – that cultural groups are relatively unproblematic entities: 'there is a group, named X, which has given boundaries and a certain culture and social structure within those limits'. The question of how those boundaries were constituted and re-constituted or the idea that the culture of the group might change while the boundary remained did not really enter into the picture.

Interethnic relations in Chiapas

An illustration of these tendencies can be found in an article by Ben Colby and Pierre van den Berghe (1961) on ethnic relations in Chiapas, southern Mexico. This is an interesting article, because it is constructed partly in opposition to the preceding functionalist, pluralist trend, while it also explicitly retains some of its ideas and its more hidden assumptions. The authors give a detailed picture of the social structure of San Cristóbal de las Casas, a colonial town and regional centre of Chiapas, and they include some of the surrounding rural area with its indian communities. The inhabitants of San Cristóbal mostly call themselves ladinos and are ranked by class; higher class people are whiter, lower class people are darker and more 'indian-looking'. The indians as such, however, do not live in the town – where they become 'rapidly ladinoised' – but in the rural areas. Socially, ladinos rank higher than indians in all respects.

Ladinos and indians also have different cultures and Colby and van den Berghe list these in a table that summarises differences in religious orientations, social relationships, family relationships, attitudes to work and so on. In a typically pluralist vein, these differences are underlain by basic forces of integration, institutions in which everyone participates: the Catholic Church, local and federal government (although the data the authors supply tend to undermine the idea of the latter as an integrative influence, since local government is entirely in the hands of the ladinos, while the local programmes of the Instituto Nacional Indigenista are run by a national administration), and the regional economy in which ladinos buy indians' goods (at exploitative prices) and indians and ladinos 'exchange services' (that is, the former work for the latter at low rates of pay). These economic exchanges are 'one of the major foci integrating ladino and Indian cultures' (p. 780).

Ladino–indian relations are described as paternalistic – presaging the comparative treatment of race relations that van den Berghe would later publish (1967) that distinguished between competitive and paternalistic forms of race and ethnic relations. This means that indians act submissively and are treated with benign condescension if they know their place. This results in a degree of social segregation, since ladinos and indians never interact on equal terms. However, relations of godparenthood, for example, cross such boundaries as indians seek ladinos to be godparents to their children. Indians can 'pass' into the ladino group by speaking good Spanish and dressing and behaving like a ladino; they may then 'still be called an Indian', but will be treated as ladinos (p. 783). This ambiguity is not clarified by the authors, although it is difficult to see how being treated as a ladino could include being called an indian when the status implications of such a label are so strong. Overall, because the ethnic line is flexible, they foresee a gradual move from this paternalistic system, inherited from the colonial past, to an 'integrated, mestizo-hispanic society' (p. 789). In contrast, in some areas of Guatemala, the ethnic line is more rigid and this creates a more competitive situation as some indians get wealthier, but are not allowed to cross the ethnic line.

This all gives quite a useful picture of ethnic relations and, as they note, it parallels to a great extent the accounts given by Tax, Gillin, Tumin and Redfield of Guatemala. However, there are a number of problems. First, each group is reified as a fairly homogeneous entity with its own culture, the traits of which can be enumerated in a table. It is implied that moving from one group to the other means a switch in cultural traits. The possibility that indians who pass into the lower class of the ladino group retain some of their cultural traits is not envisaged nor is the idea that culture might change while ethnic boundaries persist. Second, the ladino group is admitted to be highly class stratified in a way that itself mirrors a ladino–indian divide – that is, the poor ladinos are all 'indian-looking' – but this apparently has no effect on how upper-class ladinos treat lower class ones, nor how lower-class ladinos treat indians (some of whom, for example, must be their kinsfolk). We are asked to believe that all ladinos treat all indians in the same way.

Third, the ladino–indian boundary is shown to be permeable, but the way the boundary itself persists remains unclear. The boundary is assumed to exist of its own accord, but it must be the case that it is maintained by the actions of individuals who make identifications. The behaviour of lower class ladinos towards indians thus becomes crucial, but as already noted, it is not dealt with. The reasons for the persistence of the boundary in the form it does are also unclear. Putting aside the statement that the differences in ethnic relations observable between Chiapas and northern Guatemala derive 'from a difference in the flexibility in the ethnic line' (p. 787) – which appears to be a tautology, since the differences in ethnic relations *are about* the flexibility in that line – the only solid explanation given is that in Mexico a policy of cultural assimilation has existed since the 1910–17 revolution thus making passing a relatively acceptable tactic. The idea that the boundary may still exist, whatever its flexibility, because it is economically advantageous for ladinos to exploit indians is not entertained. Fourth, the authors note that the modernisation programmes of the Instituto Nacional Indigenista have been strongest in the indian villages nearest San Cristóbal, but that it is precisely these villages that have shown 'reactive resistance' and have maintained cultural distinctiveness (p. 778). This observation is left in the air, but it shows that modernisation does not necessarily lead to ladinoisation, as their analysis would suppose; it also indicates that elements of culture can change while leaving the ethnic line intact or even strengthened and it undermines their optimistic prediction of a move towards an 'integrated mestizo-hispanic society' as indians rise in education and wealth. Finally, although the activities of the INI are discussed, there is little sense of the place of indians as a category in the nation-state or of how local hierarchies reproduce national ones.

In sum, then, this analysis still carries within a large quantity of functionalist baggage. Van den Berghe was soon to change and, after a period working in South Africa, and influenced no doubt by the less benign visions of pluralism produced by M.G. Smith for the Caribbean (1965) and Leo Kuper for South Africa (Kuper and Smith, 1969), his own approach moved away from functionalism, although he retained the concept of pluralism (see next chapter). Others also began to see ethnic identity as more flexible and not destined to disappear with development. Hinshaw's 1964 restudy of a community in Guatemala, first studied by Tax in 1937, showed that 'Panajacheleños [had] acculturated in these respects [of dress, language and employment] while remaining Indian in identity' (Tax and Hinshaw, 1970: 192). Nash (1958) had already found similar patterns, but his argument that industrial technology did not mean cultural disintegration in an indian community was directed more at proving that indians were amenable to modernisation – along the lines of Tax's (1953) argument that Guatemalan indians were 'penny capitalists' – than at showing the contextual nature of ethnic identity.

The analysis of colonialism

There were also important currents within Mexico at this time – which in the late 1960s and 1970s found echo in Peru (where several Mexican anthropologists did research) – that went against the functionalist flow (Hewitt de Alcántara, 1984: ch. 2). The driving force here was an analysis of colonialism which was being undertaken especially in Britain and France, in the context of post-war decolonisation, but had also been part of the Marxist-influenced radical thought of the Peruvians José Carlos Mariátegui and Víctor Raúl Haya de la Torre in the 1920s and 1930s that influenced scholars all over Latin America. Mexicans Gonzalo Aguirre Beltrán and Julio de la Fuente were among those who, according to van den Berghe (1974b: 2), arrived at a 'happy marriage of Marxist class theory and Chicago anthropology' and this allowed them to emphasise inequality and exploitation while also dealing with ethnic and racial identities.

47

Julio de la Fuente – who started out as a Marxist, was attracted by functionalism and indeed worked with that founding father of functionalism, Malinowski, on a study of Mexican markets in the early 1940s (Drucker-Brown, 1982) – worked on interethnic relations in the Chiapas region and came to the conclusion that the label 'indian' was a tool used by mestizos to ascribe inferior status to those perceived as different and thus legitimate their exploitation (de la Fuente, 1965; Hewitt de Alcántara, 1984: 46–8). In the 1950s and 1960s, Aguirre Beltrán developed the concept of regions of refuge. As with de la Fuente, there was a strong Marxist influence in his work and he focused on unequal exploitative relations between urban and rural dwellers in rather isolated regions. In these 'refuge regions', urban dwellers used ascriptions of indian identity to legitimate social stratification: 'the class struggle between the elite and the illiterate masses takes on the tones of an interethnic battle' (Aguirre Beltrán, 1979: 93).

In both these approaches, there is an implicit challenge to the assumption that the boundary between indian and mestizo, and the categories it separates, are just 'there', as pre-constituted objective facts to be investigated. The implication, albeit not really explored by either scholar, is that both are constructed in processes of exploitation and unequal exchange. This prefigured the 'instrumentalist' approach to ethnicity that I outlined in Chapter 1. Nevertheless, some of the same problems emerge as with the functionalists: not enough attention is paid to the way the boundary is constructed and maintained; the implication is that all mestizos exploit all indians in a way that sits ill at ease with the realities of boundary-crossing. There is thus a tendency – as in other analyses of 'the colonial situation' – to create two static homogeneous groups of colonisers and colonised: as Aguirre Beltrán said for the Chiapas region, 'social mobility scarcely exists' (1979: 93), a comment which fails to capture any sense of process. Also, partly due to the Marxist influence, there is the problem of 'reducing' these ethnic and racial identifications to economic determinants, thus denying them their own dynamics.

Blacks: Integration in a Class Society

As with indians, one way of approaching blacks was as a 'problem' in processes of nation-building and, as with indians, this overlapped strongly, especially among Latin American academics, with the scientific study of blacks as bearers of particular ways of life. The latter occurred first in countries that had large and culturally quite distinctive black populations, principally Cuba and Brazil which had both continued to purchase African slaves as late as the 1870s (Curtin, 1969: 234), with slavery persisting into the last decades of the nineteenth century. In other countries, such as Colombia and Venezuela, blacks were considered within the general perspective of the future of the nation and its racial constitution, but were not a focus of study until later (Wade, 1993a; Wright, 1990).

Among the first specialists on blacks were Raimundo Nina Rodrigues in Brazil and Fernando Ortiz in Cuba – the latter for example published an important study in 1906. Both scholars were, at this stage, deeply enmeshed in the scientific racism of the day. Ortiz was engaged on a long-term study of Afro-Cuban criminality and underworld culture, the aim of which was to investigate these with a view to eliminating them as backward elements in the nation's progress. Ortiz clearly saw Afro-Cubans as inferior at this early stage of his career. Phrenology – the study that drew a link between head form and aspects of character – was popular at the time as part of the more fringe domains of racial science and the Italian phrenologist Cesare Lombroso contributed a preface to Ortiz's first book on Afro-Cuban criminality (Ortiz, 1973 [1906]; see also Ortiz, 1984).

In Brazil, the early studies of medic Nina Rodrigues – himself a mulatto – made him 'the most prestigious doctrinaire Brazilian racist of his era' until he died in 1906 (Skidmore, 1974: 58). His legacy was soon overshadowed, first by the physician Arthur Ramos, who published on Afro-Brazilian culture, and then in the 1930s by the writings of Gilberto Freyre. As mentioned in the previous chapter, Freyre became a central figure in Brazilian views on blacks and national identity. Redefining what it meant to be Brazilian was not, however, a purely inward-looking endeavour: Brazil was being represented on the international stage as well. Here Freyre was making a comparison between Brazil and the US that was a vital part of Brazil's self-image and, for decades to come, of academic writing about comparative race relations in the Americas.

Freyre was claiming that Brazil was, compared to the US, a 'racial democracy'. This argument, as made by Freyre or as developed later, held that slavery had been more benign in Brazil, the Portuguese colonists more tolerant of race mixture, abolition had been less disruptive and contested, there was no strict segregation, no lynching, and so on. This led to a more tolerant, mixed society that, while it might be strongly divided by class, was 'with respect to race relations ... probably the nearest approach to paradise to be found anywhere in the world' (1959: 9). Frank Tannenbaum added scholarly weight to this argument in his book *Slave and Citizen* (1948) which argued that Iberian slave law (which allowed manumission) and the influence of the Catholic church had both helped integrate blacks into Latin American slave societies in ways that contrasted with Anglo-Saxon America. There has been great debate about whether slavery was, in fact, more benign in Latin America than in the US or, say, Jamaica and the upshot has been that it was impossible to generalise in these broad terms; too much depended on local factors (Davis, 1969; Graham, 1970; Lombardi, 1974). Still, it was undeniable that, in Latin America generally (i) blacks were freed more frequently than in the southern US; (ii) race mixture was more common; and (iii) the products of that mixture were recognised as socially distinct from their parents. In contrast, in the US, (i) freedom for blacks was limited and highly controlled; (ii) race mixture occurred, but was repressed; and (iii) the offspring of mixed unions were not really accorded a social space of their own: the early recognition of a mixed, 'mulatto' category was partial and evaporated during the nineteenth century so that mulattoes were basically classified as blacks.

Harris (1974) thought that Tannenbaum was wrong about the law and the Church and that the reasons for these differences were economic and political. In Brazil, the lack of a solid indian population meant Africans were the main workforce, but there was a labour market gap, so to speak, between white masters and slaves. This was best filled by freed slaves who, as it happened, were generally mixed, since the mulatto children of white men with slave women were obvious candidates for being freed. Recognition of mixed people as a specific category was then a natural consequence. In the US, a plentiful supply of poor whites filled that gap and the competitive relations established between white and black ensured that the category 'black' would be heavily policed with racism and legal restrictions that tried to make all blacks slaves and deny intermediate racial categories.

Harris's argument was undermined by the existence of a recognised middle racial category in the northern European Caribbean colonies, where it did not seem to be economically necessary, but emerged perhaps more as a political buffer between a tiny white elite and a huge slave population (Jordan,

1969). Hoetink (1969) also pointed out the importance of the existence of a solid white family structure in inhibiting race mixture and, above all, the recognition of mixed people as socially different: both of these were more likely to occur where colonists tended to be single men.

Whatever the precise reasons for the emergence of the contrast (see Foner and Genovese, 1969; Wade, 1986), the point remains that it is hard to argue that some generalised tolerance was at the roots of the Latin American pattern. This pattern is, it is true, characterised by complex processes of mixture that have stopped the emergence of relatively clear US-type black–white boundaries, but, as we shall see in ensuing chapters, this does not mean that Latin America is the polar opposite of the US, as racial paradise is the opposite of racial hell. Both societies were slave societies, built on racially ranked stratification; they developed in different ways, but they also share a good deal in terms of the hierarchisation of racial identities. However, the idea of Brazil as a racial democracy that Freyre popularised has been very influential and set the agenda for much of the study of blacks in Latin America generally.

Race and class in Brazil: the UNESCO studies

One of the results of the differences explored in Chapter 2 between the status of blacks and indians in the intellectual – and especially anthropological – panorama was that there never really emerged a tradition, functionalist or otherwise, of doing intensive ethnographies that had as their object the explication of the internal characteristics of particular black communities. Although some community-based studies were done, the aim was to illuminate something about Brazilian race relations. Blacks were not seen, in the same way as indians often were, as Others to be studied in their own right, as a separate category; they were seen, as indians only sometimes were, in terms of their relations to others in the nation.

Donald Pierson's *Negroes in Brazil: A Study of Race Contact at Bahía* (1942) fits into such a trend and also into the comparative race relations approach implied in Freyre's work. Bahía as the blackest, most African-looking area of Brazil has tended to attract academic attention and Pierson found there a 'multiracial class society' (p. 336). In his view,

In Bahía there is probably little or no race prejudice in the sense in which that term is used in the United States. There are no castes based on race; there are only classes. This does not mean that there is nothing that might properly be called prejudice but that such prejudice as does exist is *class* rather than *caste* prejudice. (p. 331)

He was using the word 'caste' here as it had been used in the US to characterise the deep-seated black–white segregation of the southern US, hedged about with complex rules of etiquette that defined the appropriate behaviour between whites and blacks, irrespective of their economic status, as that between master and servant. In contrast, Pierson found that 'relations between the races in Brazil have *always been*, to a considerable extent, intimate and cordial' (p. 335, emphasis added). The putative historical depth given to this cordiality – Sérgio Buarque de Holanda had already written about the 'cordial man' as a central figure of the Brazilian national character (Linger, 1992: 8) – implies the idea of a benign Brazilian slavery and, as to the future, Pierson envisaged 'the gradual but persistent reduction of all distinguishing racial and cultural marks and the fusing, biologically and culturally, of the African and the European into one race and one common culture' (p. 337).

The problems with such an approach are manifold and more evident now that racial and ethnic identifications are clearly not disappearing. Suffice to say at this stage that Pierson had thrown the baby out with the bath water: for him, Bahía was not like the US; therefore race was more or less irrelevant. The fact that, according to his own figures, 98 per cent of blacks were in the lower class, while 86 per cent of whites were in what he called 'the intelligentsia' (that is, the upper class), had to be explained, in his approach, in terms of past discriminations (for example, of slavery) which had placed blacks at the bottom, but which now (almost magically) were purely 'class' discriminations. Racism played no further role in maintaining inequality and this was evident to Pierson because relations were 'cordial'. The possibility that racism could operate in ways different from in the US is not really explored.

It was this 'traditional' vision of Brazil purveyed by Freyre and Pierson (Toplin, 1971) that was vital when, after the horrors of Nazi racism and as part of the final dismantling of scientific racism and eugenics, UNESCO – headed at the time by Arthur Ramos – decided to undertake a study of race relations in Brazil that, within the overall UNESCO initiative on attacking racism (Barkan, 1996), would show the world how to get things right in this respect.

The UNESCO studies covered very different areas of Brazil and this is important when assessing the results of their research. One UNESCO team, headed by Charles Wagley and including Thales de Azevedo, Luiz Costa Pinto, Harry Hutchinson, Marvin Harris and Ben Zimmerman, focused on northeast and central Brazil, including Rio. Another team, headed by Roger Bastide and Florestan Fernandes and including Oracy Nogueira, focused on southern Brazil, especially São Paulo. In this latter region, the black presence was more recent and there was a large white population, much of which was of relatively recent European origin; race relations there were arguably more conflictive than in the northeast where Pierson had also worked. Also Fernandes was more radical in his views than many of the northern team; he later became part of the so-called São Paulo school, with Fernando Henrique Cardoso and Octavio Ianni, which was purged from São Paulo university by the military government in 1969.

The results of the UNESCO studies varied a good deal, but overall there was little evidence to sustain the idea of a racial democracy. Most researchers reported evidence of racial prejudice and discrimination (for example, Azevedo, 1953; Bastide and Fernandes, 1955; Nogueira, 1955; Wagley, 1952). Rather than attempting to summarise all these studies – which have been reviewed in Bastide (1957), Banton (1967), Graham (1970) and Fontaine (1980) – I will look in some detail at a couple of significant examples.

Marvin Harris carried out an anthropological study of the town of Minas Velhas in Minas Gerais (Harris, 1952). In this study he detailed at length the negative and racist stereotypes that surrounded the image of *negro* in the town, but then explained that whites never actually behaved on the basis of these stereotypes because there was 'no status-role for the Negro as Negro, nor for the white as white' (1952: 63). That is, the image of *negro* was an ideal type that did not correspond to a real individual; there was no actual category of people agreed to be *negros*; the term was virtually an insult and the word *preto* was more commonly used for dark-skinned people. In reality, people's status was determined by a number of criteria – mainly wealth and occupation – of which racial identification was only one. Here the implicit comparison with the US is clear: an opposition was set up between a system in which the racial criterion did define everything (the US 'caste' system in which, as Malcolm X so pithily put it, a black PhD was still called a 'nigger') and one in which it was merely one factor among others (the Brazil 'class' system).

Harris then looked in more detail at the social structure of the town and defined three ranked groups on the basis of wealth and occupation. These, he said, represented the town's actual status groups – they defined who associated with whom on equal social terms. He then analysed whether race could place a person in a different group from that for which their wealth and occupation qualified them. He found that race was a secondary diagnostic in that this almost never happened: there was only one black man who qualified economically for Group A status but was denied full social participation in it because he was black (p. 68). However, he admitted that, since race and class criteria overlapped so much, this did not actually tell us much. That is, each group was more or less homogeneous with respect to both economic and racial criteria: only four per cent of the top group were non-white, while only 20 per cent of the bottom group were white (p. 70). Thus to say *rico* (rich) was the same as saying *branco* (white), while *pobre* (poor) and *preto* were also virtually synonymous. Harris went on to say that, in the middle group, there was evidence that racial criteria were creating a split. People in that group divided over their basic identification with the rich whites as against the poor blacks. This was evident, for example, in the creation of competing carnival celebrations for *brancos-ricos* and *pretos-pobres* which tended to split the middle group. Thus there was 'no justification for dismissing race as a chimerical side-effect of the class structure' (p. 77).

Harris's study was flawed in a number of ways. He admitted that the overlap between race and class severely undermined the whole procedure of assessing race as a diagnostic of rank. A better way of proceeding might have been to define status groups independently, simply on the basis of who associated with whom on equal terms, and then see how homogeneous these groups were with respect to race and class criteria. Even this would have come up against the same problem, but we might then have known more about what happened with the significant minority of whites in the bottom class: how did they treat the blacks and mulattoes in their class? Did they have greater chances of upward economic mobility because they were white and might get favourable treatment from richer whites? Harris's analysis is too static (and indeed the economy of the town itself was too stagnant) to answer such crucial questions.

Nevertheless, Harris went on to make more sweeping statements about race in Brazil, for example in *Patterns of Race in the*

Americas, first published in 1964. Here he said that, 'the issue of racial discrimination is scarcely a vital one' and that 'as far as behaviour is concerned, "races" do not exist for the Brazilians' (1974: 63, 64). Yet Thales de Azevedo, working in Bahía, had concluded that 'coloured people are still considered to be part of a biological and social category characterised by traits thought to be inferior to those of whites' (1953: 103, my translation). For Harris, class was the main factor in ranking: 'It is class which determines who will be admitted to hotels, restaurants and social clubs' (1974: 61). Yet in 1951, the black US dancer, Katherine Dunham, had complained of being refused admittance to a São Paulo hotel and the ensuing fuss had led to the passage of the Afonso Arinos Law prohibiting such discrimination (Skidmore, 1974: 212). Azevedo had also found that 'often blacks do not encounter barriers because, knowing the prejudices of the whites, they avoid certain places' (1953: ch. 7, my translation).

Harris (1970) also argued that Brazilian modes of racial classification led to the 'maximization of ambiguity': there were dozens of terms commonly used to classify people by their appearance and the same individual might be classified in different ways by different people. This was in contrast to the US where racial terminology was simpler and more agreed upon. Since 'the *sine qua non* of any thorough-going minority system is a foolproof method of separating a population into superordinate and subordinate groups' (Harris, 1974: 54), Brazil could not have such a system. The problems here are, first, that although many terms are used to classify people in Brazil, and elsewhere in Latin America, other research indicates that, in practice, people operate with basic conceptual prototypical categories for ordering that variety that correspond roughly to black, white and indian and the first-level mixtures between these three (Sanjek, 1971; Whitten, 1985: 42). Second, it is true that there is not a 'thorough-going minority system' in Brazil or elsewhere in Latin America, but this hardly clarifies the role that race evidently does play. As with Pierson, the baby is being thrown out with the bathwater.

Fernandes (1969) was more emphatic about the existence of racism in São Paulo society and this book, which drew on the research done in the 1950s, documented in detail how blacks and whites felt about each other and about racism. However, the detail of the work – which in any case is rather abstract, since there is little concrete ethnography and many decontextualised anecdotes and interviews – is set within Fernandes's overall understanding of race and capitalism. He saw an overall process in which slavery placed blacks and mulattoes – Fernandes did not distinguish greatly between these categories – at the bottom of the social hierarchy. Abolition occurred under the pressures of capitalist expansion and the demand for free labour. Freed blacks were not integrated, however, due to their lack of education and skills necessary for the capitalist labour market, or as Fernandes called it 'the competitive social order'. The heavy white immigration that occurred in southern Brazil between 1880 and 1930 merely exacerbated this situation, displacing blacks from the labour market and causing a stage of marginality in which alcoholism, crime, broken families and so on undermined even more their ability to compete. Nevertheless, immigration expanded the competitive social order, bringing modernisation and, over time, the gradual integration of blacks.

Fernandes saw, then, a gradual shift from a traditional society based on paternalism, with blacks 'knowing their place', towards a democratic capitalism within which racial discrimination would have no function; racial identities would decline in the face of class. The racism that Fernandes documented so carefully was, in his view, an anachronism, a hold-over from previous times, but it would remain unless there was proactive effort on the part of whites to remove it; white indifference was also to blame for lack of black integration. The result that he found in the 1950s was what he called a system of 'accommodation' (1969: 391): individualistic mobility was permitted for a small number of blacks and mulattoes, while the rest remained in the lower strata, kept in place by negative stereotypes and racial discrimination, by white indifference and by the lack of a concerted political challenge by blacks and mulattoes. Racial prejudice was usually dissimulated and many blacks (especially those who accepted their place in the system) themselves denied its existence. Those blacks who did achieve some upward mobility tended to distance themselves from other blacks, associating with and perhaps marrying white people; this too made black political mobilisation difficult.

There are clearly problems with Fernandes's idea that there is an overall shift in progress from a traditional to a modern society in which racial identity is, by definition, irrelevant. Bastide (1957) was less sanguine and saw a continuing role for racism in a competitive society, a position also taken by van den Berghe (1967: ch. 3). Nevertheless, the details of his analysis of the practice of accommodation capture, in my view, many salient aspects of racial identifications in Brazil and elsewhere. To take just one example, accommodation serves, in his view, to mask the realities of racial prejudice. In 1995, the São Paulo newspaper, *Folha*, carried out a national survey on attitudes to race. One question asked people who identified themselves as blacks and mulattoes if they had ever been subject to discrimination; 77 per cent said no (although this was 64 per cent for blacks alone).[1] In my experience in Colombia, some blacks denied being discriminated against because to admit this was, in their view, to admit to being the type of person who might be discriminated against – not only black, but, by association, untrustworthy, stupid and so on – as if it might be their fault that they were discriminated against (Wade, 1993a: ch. 13).

There is, however, a strong tendency in Fernandes's work to take 'black' and 'mulatto' as unproblematic categories. Harris goes too far in using the ambiguity of classification to argue for the irrelevance of racial identities, but the blurring of racial categories, their contextual nature and the whole ideology of 'whitening' which valorises whiteness and opens the limited possibility of black and mulatto people renegotiating their own and their children's racial identity, are vital aspects of the situation in Brazil and elsewhere that are suggested, but that do not receive the attention they need in Fernandes's work.

In sum, then, the UNESCO studies undermined the idea of a racial democracy in Brazil and, in some cases, detailed many aspects of how racism worked in a non-US, non-'caste' system. However, there was still a tendency to deny the significance of race or to see it as declining over time: Brazil was basically a class society. I think it has not been sufficiently recognised in the literature on these studies that these conclusions were almost always in implicit comparison with the US: the latter's 'caste' system was the home of 'real' race relations and racism against which other societies could be measured. The idea that one could think in terms of different forms of racism and race relations without necessarily opposing them was not easily entertained. There was also a general tendency in these studies to reify racial categories (Fernandes) or to deny them completely for the Brazilian case (Harris); the idea that racial categories are in a constant process of re-constitution through people's practice and exist contextually and interactively was not current, and it was this that gave rise to some of the problems in seeing what racial identities meant in Brazil. Since they were not like those in the US – where their reification by analysts was understandable given their relative social solidity – they somehow eluded observers' analytical grasp.

Conclusion

There are two main trends underlying these early studies that I want to highlight. First, the idea that racial and ethnic identities were destined to disappear: this was evident in much intellectual thought, including that of some *indigenistas*, about the nation. This was a general tendency at the time, but in Latin America especially, the association of blacks and indians with the past has been very strong: they have been associated with primitivism, slavery, antique modes of production, traditionalism and so on. Even the trends in *indigenismo* and *negrismo* that sprung up in the 1920s and 1930s (see Chapter 2) were mostly based on valuing these traits, rather than challenging them. The idea, argued by Gilroy (1993a), that blacks in the Atlantic diaspora have been in the vanguard of modernity – prefiguring its crises of identity and critiquing its contradictions – was barely conceivable.

The second trend is the taking for granted of racial and ethnic identities. These were generally conceived as being concrete things 'on the ground' which could be put under the microscope. People might pass from one to another or one might argue that they did not exist except as 'mere' ideas (as did Harris, 1952), but in general there was an impoverished analysis of the relation between ideas and practice – groups existed and people had ideas and feelings about them. The interactive, recursive relation between the groups as perpetually re-constituted collectivities in action and the groups as perpetually re-imagined communities in thought was not grasped.

4. INEQUALITY AND SITUATIONAL IDENTITY: 1970s

Dependency and Situational Ethnicity

By the middle of the 1960s, the growing influence of radical perspectives in social science was apparent. Marxism had been a constant presence in Latin American social science – as I showed in the previous chapter, it had influenced writers from José Carlos Mariátegui in 1920s' Peru to Aguirre Beltrán in 1960s' Mexico – but it now took on new force, often channelled through ideas about dependency which could be more or less distant from classical Marxism.

Dependency theory had emerged after the war and incorporated various different strands in Latin America. On the one hand, there was the analysis of unequal terms of trade associated with Raúl Prébisch and the Economic Commission for Latin America; this position, which was not really a Marxist one, argued that Latin America was disadvantaged by unfavourable terms of trade with Europe and the US and needed economic protection to allow more independent industrial development. On the other hand, there was the Marxist analysis of imperialism which, as developed by Lenin, Rudolf Hilferding and Rosa Luxemburg, related imperial expansion directly to the internal dynamics of the capitalist mode of production. This was the kind of approach developed by André Gunder Frank who, concentrating more on capitalist exchange than production, understood the poverty of the Third World as a result of the expropriation of resources from the periphery, through a chain of exploitative metropolis–satellite relations, to the centre. This is not the place to enter into an assessment of development theory (see Kay, 1989), but the point is that inequality and mechanisms of exploitation were an increasingly important focus of attention for those whose gaze had been fixed on smaller domains of interethnic relations. Thus, during the 1970s and into the next decade, many debates centred on the relative roles of class and ethnicity or race.

At the same time, the analysis of ethnicity was advanced by anthropologists such as Frederick Barth (1969), Abner Cohen (1969, 1974) and Epstein (1978). This established ethnic identity as a more flexible, contextual construct and worked against the tendency to reify social groups that had been common. In the introduction to his edited collection (1969), Barth argued that ethnic groups were socially constructed and that the focus of analysis should be the boundaries of the group. He criticised the current conception of ethnic groups as self-perpetuating entities with given sets of cultural attributes. He emphasised that ethnic groups exist *in relation to* others; people establish boundaries on the basis of criteria that seem important to them, whether or not an outside observer can appreciate these differences. Boundaries continue to exist when people and cultural information cross them and they may have a different character depending on what differences are being emphasised by the actors concerned in a given situation. Although Barth himself did, at times, suggest that ethnic identity was, in the end, a rather inflexible, permanent aspect of a person (Banks, 1996: 13–14), he established the basis for seeing ethnic identity as *situational*: if it is established in relation to something else, then it will vary depending on what that something is.

In short, then, both these overall trends moved away from the emphasis on 'isolated' communities in functionalist anthropology and located ethnic groups more in the context of the nation and in history, and more in terms of economic inequality and social constructedness. Ethnic identities were also understood as phenomena that were not necessarily destined to fade away with 'modernisation'; being flexible and being connected to inequality, there was no inherent drive for their disappearance.

Indians: Ethnicity, Dependency and Resistance

Some of the changes that occurred in this period can be judged by looking again at Pierre van den Berghe. In 1969, Colby and he published *Ixil Country: A Plural Society in Highland Guatemala* which retained the pluralist approach they had used before, but was now tempered with a greater emphasis on economic and political domination. Ethnic boundaries were related not only to the way that people cooperated and exchanged services, but also to the way that one group dominated another. Van den Berghe then moved his area of research to Peru where he studied the community of San Jerónimo, near Cuzco.

In one article on the subject (1975), he begins with the uncompromising statement that 'throughout the world, the practical import of ethnicity is intimately linked with the unequal distribution of power and wealth' (p. 71). He avoids, however, any tendency to assume that class is automatically more significant than ethnicity. Van den Berghe then outlines the 'sociology of dependence approach' as elaborated by Peruvian researchers such as Fernando Fuenzalida and José Matos Mar, according to which 'Peruvian social structure is conceived as a multitude of binary relations of dependence and domination', forming 'chains of dependence' that 'converge at the apex into the national, and beyond it, the international ruling oligarchy' (p. 73; see also Long, 1977: ch. 4; van den Berghe 1974a: 16). Indianness, in this scheme, is defined as 'the low end of a dependency chain on nearly all dimensions of unequal relations' (p. 74). The strength of this approach, for van den Berghe, is that ethnicity is anchored in power relations; thus culture does not by itself define ethnic boundaries, since it is impossible in Peru neatly to separate indian from mestizo culture; rather, power differences define that boundary. He admits that this approach 'tends to submerge ethnicity too much under class', resulting in the attempt, for example, to understand indians as peasants rather than indians (p. 75). He emphasises that there are specifically cultural aspects to the situation – for example, ethnic difference makes the system of domination 'all the more difficult to shake' (p. 77); or there are the local power-brokers of indian origin who use their knowledge of Quechua the better to manipulate their former peers (p. 77).

Ethnic boundaries in general should, in van den Berghe's view, be defined both objectively (in terms of objective cultural traits) and subjectively (in terms of what people say they are) – elsewhere van den Berghe rejects what he takes to be Barth's extreme subjectivist position (actually less so than he suspects) which, he says, argues that 'an ethnic group is whatever anybody says it is' (1974b: 5). In Peru, however, ethnic boundaries are to a great extent 'defined subjectively, relatively and situationally' (1975: 73). Thus the upper class of San Jerónimo might be seen as mestizo by local standards, but as *cholo* by the upper class of Cuzco; the term *cholo* does not define a group of people, but is a relational term, used to deprecate individuals that the speaker sees as inferior. Likewise, there is little consensus as to who is mestizo and who indian, with some people classing most others in the town as mestizos and others labelling them indians. This, however, is not very typical of the Andes and in many other areas the indian–mestizo line is much more sharply drawn (p. 82). In any event, although boundaries are flexible in this way, important differences of power and wealth are evident in the town and these correspond to ethnic differences: indian is low status, mestizo is higher.

Van den Berghe retains, however, an important element of his previous position: Peru's is a relatively open system which allows 'considerable mobility' from the indian group to the mestizo group and in which, therefore, 'the subordinate group steadily decreases in proportion' (1975: 83, 78). The fact that this seems to contradict his idea that the indian–mestizo boundary is maintained by power relations rather than cultural difference is not addressed, unless the (unlikely) argument is that the hierarchy of these power relations is itself diminishing.

François Bourricaud was less positive about the future of Peruvian society. In an important article (1975), he is critical of dependency theory because the simple fact of dependence cannot explain the peculiarities of Peru 'which is a mixture of very heterogeneous elements strangely combining great rigidity with great fluidity'. This is why, he says, 'the cholo emerges as a key character': it is the *cholo* who 'represents the element of mobility in a system which neither encourages nor stresses mobility' (1975: 357). Ultimately, however, Peru cannot crystallise as a nation around either the symbol of *cholo* (which is too pejorative a term), or indian or mestizo; in Peru there is neither a class nor a caste system, there is only heterogeneous change, the direction of which Bourricaud admits he is uncertain about (1975: 386).

Rodolfo Stavenhagen was also more cautious in his views – this time with reference to the Chiapas highlands. He saw relations of colonialism and class co-existing over a long period of time as aspects of stratified interethnic relations. Class relations were tending to displace colonial ones, but this did not necessarily mean the erasure of indian ethnic identity. He mentioned the persistence of 'Indian cultural identity independent of stratification' (1975: 206) which occurred when indians moved up in the ranking system without loss of identity. In addition, the loss of ethnic identity by indians could be interpreted as a negative move, heralding proletarianisation and even marginalisation rather than upward mobility (1975: 215).

Judith Friedlander, working in Mexico, addressed the logic of van den Berghe's argument about culture, but in a different way. In her view, indian culture in Hueyapan was constantly changing, taking on traits that were being discarded by the Mexican upper classes as they redefined their identity and acquired new symbols. But

> despite the fact that the 'content' of Hueyapan culture is always changing, the 'structural' relationship of Indian to hispanic remains the same. The villagers are still Indians by virtue of the fact that they continue to lack what the elite continues to acquire.

Meanwhile the Hueyapeños themselves 'do not make the distinction between their "culture", which has been changing, and their "class", which has remained virtually the same'; they see their culture as basically the same as during colonial times (1975: 71). Friedlander's and van den Berghe's views of indian culture as a changeable, flexible construct thus contrast with the image of indian culture as static, conservative and traditional that was a corollary of George Foster's notion of 'limited good'. That some people, including indians themselves, might *see* indian culture as static and traditional is true, but this puts the issue on a different footing, opening up a more complex approach to competing discourses about indian culture (see Chapter 7).

Ideas about the persistence of ethnic boundaries despite cultural change and the consequent possibility of ethnic identities that might persist in a changing form were also reflected in studies done on urban migrants. The process of urbanisation had been widely assumed to lead to cultural homogenisation and the submergence of 'traditional' ethnic identities into urban class identity; urbanisation was, after all, seen to be a central dynamic in modernisation. Research by Roberts (1974), Doughty (1972), Isbell (1978: ch. 8) indicated that this was not necessarily the case, showing that strong links between city and village often existed and that rituals and festivals from village life were adapted to city settlements. This indicated cultural continuities, but said little about ethnic identification. In fact, self-identification as indian or perhaps *cholo* among migrants was generally avoided, since these terms were associated with the rural backwardness that most migrants wished to avoid at all costs. However, these labels did not disappear. Bourricaud (1975: 384) argued that in Lima terms such as indian and *cholo* were used by some migrants to describe other migrants; and none of these migrants would 'be recognised by anyone outside their own circles as anything other than cholos' (see also Radcliffe, 1990). Categorisations based on perceived cultural (and doubtless physical) differences were thus still an important part of everyday urban life.

Internal colonialism and resistance

Directly connected to dependency approaches and the analysis of colonialism was the development of theories of internal colonialism. One of the first to use the idea was the Mexican Pablo González Casanova, building on Aguirre Beltrán's notion of region of refuge (see Chapter 3). The idea was simply that relations of exploitation between regions within a country paralleled those between colonising and colonised countries: the existence of a territorial distinction; the monopolisation of trade and (sometimes) control of production in the colonised territory by an external elite, which was ethnically and/or racially distinct; the control of the colony's institutions by that elite; and the subordination of the colonised population in political, economic and cultural terms to the coloniser's priorities (González Casanova, 1971; Hechter, 1975; van den Berghe, 1974b: 6). The difference from the region of refuge idea was that the internal colony was not an isolated backward region, dominated by a local elite, that could be modernised through integration into the nation; rather it was already integrated into national and international circuits of capitalist production and exchange (Hewitt de Alcántara, 1984: 113). The idea that exploitation was the driving force behind ethnic and racial distinctions was, however, very much the same.

The theory of internal colonialism was used extensively to characterise the position of indian communities or regions in Latin America. Norman Whitten used it, for example, in his analysis of Ecuadorian jungle Quichua on the borders between Amazonia and the Andes (1975, 1976). These people were not homogeneous, but had a clear self-identification which was becoming clearer, not merging with mestizo culture: 'Lowland Quechua ethnicity [has to be understood] as a rational response to expanding opportunities in the money economy under the continuance of internal colonialism in Ecuador' (1975: 47).[1]

Whitten (1976) focuses on an indian *comuna* (roughly, a reserve) established in 1947, near the growing colonist town of

Puyo. The *comuna* was established by the state partly to offset foreign encroachment; the land around it quickly passed into private ownership by mestizo colonists: as such the *comuna* represents 'a special aspect of national expansion and, increasingly, a basis for indigenous survival' (p. 240). Whitten uses the concept of internal colonialism partly because of the special legal status of the *comuna* which creates a separate territory within the nation and because of the strong racial ideology of mixedness as the basic characteristic of Ecuadorian national identity which is 'a powerful mechanism for exclusion of the non-mixed' (pp. 251, 275); thus mestizos – who may identify as *blancos* (whites) in the local context to further differentiate themselves from indians – are the colonisers of indian territory. The labelling of indians by mestizos creates an expanding generalised category of *indio* to which mestizos contrast themselves, especially when competing for economic opportunities. Mestizos use the categorisation to block the access of those they label as indian to strategic resources and this, plus the overall process of ethnocide which affects the Quichua, forces their ethnic identity to intensify in a corresponding process of 'ethnogenesis' (p. 281). In doing so, however, the Quichua fall more definitively under the aegis of 'protective' national policy on indians which is in fact rather restrictive compared to state policy encouraging colonisation of 'undeveloped' regions through infrastructural expansion. Here, then, we see at least three sets of actors defining the ethnic boundary: the state with its definition of the indian *comuna*, the colonists and the indians. Indians are culturally distinct – although they wear western clothes, avoid face-painting and feather-wearing when with mestizos and speak Quichua which is understood by many non-indians (p. 278) – but it is not this that maintains the ethnic boundary; this is a product of political and economic relations.

Internal colonialism was not actually a vital feature of Whitten's argument and in his edited volume on Ecuador (1981a) it received only a passing mention, although many of the same ideas as before characterise the chapters in this volume. Elsewhere, the 'theory' of internal colonialism remained rather vague, liable to be applied as a metaphor to any situation of exploitation that displayed ethnic or racial dimensions and liable also to overemphasise the internal homogeneity of colonisers and colonised and the rigidity of the boundary separating them (Stone, 1979; Wolpe, 1975). Yet it enjoyed a certain vogue precisely because of its focus on economic exploitation alongside ethnic and racial discrimination, even if the relationship between these remained rather under-theorised and ultimately reductive: ethnic identities became the mere products of economic relations; culture as a value *in its own right*, with which people might mobilise, define themselves and come into conflict, was not really embraced.

With the analysis of colonialism came the analysis of resistance. Whitten broached this in his work on the jungle Quichua – in so far as he saw the indians as struggling to defend their land and interests – and similar concerns were voiced by others. Previously, there had been a tendency to see indian or peasant resistance as a supposedly traditional, conservative resistance to modernisation and national incorporation. Now it began to be seen as a positive thing, the resistance of an oppressed minority against political and cultural domination. In her ethnography of Chuschi, an indian 'closed corporate community' in the Peruvian Andes, Billie Jean Isbell (1978) investigates 'the structural defences the indigenous population has constructed against the increasing domination of the outside world' (p. 11). She takes the idea of internal colonialism as a theoretical basis for her work (p. 19), but it does not figure in much detail: the point is simply to emphasise political and economic inequality and to locate the village in the national context, rather than seeing it as an isolate in the old functionalist fashion.

The central conflict in the village is between 'the communal members' ideology of self-sufficiency and the increasing pressures toward cultural and economic incorporation into the nation' (p. 11). This is expressed mainly through a division between *comuneros*, the indian insiders, and the *vecinos* (literally, neighbours), the mestizo foreigners resident in the village who include the shopkeepers, bureaucrats, teachers and the priest. The fundamental distinction between them is not dress or language or 'outward orientation to the Peruvian nation', it is accepting or negating 'membership in the commune with all of the attendant obligations' (p. 73); these involve the reciprocal exchange of labour and participation in certain activities and rituals, including ones in which the insider–outsider boundary is dramatised. Ethnic boundaries are maintained by different sets of activities and by fairly rigid labelling: Isbell reports universal agreement on who belongs in which category (p. 73).

These mechanisms of differentiation constitute a 'defence' against the outside world in the sense of a barrier rather than a positive strategy. More direct tactics are employed by the migrants from the village to Lima, and by return migrants. The migrants in Lima formed a society which intervenes in village politics, organising the village's communal council, removing a disliked mestizo school director, trying to turn Church lands into a village cooperative and in general mediating between national bureaucracy and the village. The migrants have an ambivalent status in the village, since they are seen as insiders and outsiders, urban and rural, beneficial for the village, but also trying to control it for their own ends. They occupy the bureaucratic posts once held by vecinos, but identify themselves as *comuneros* or 'sons of *comuneros*' (p. 193) – there must be flexibility here in ethnic identifications that belies Isbell's more rigid depictions of the *vecino–comunero* boundary.

Both Isbell and Whitten saw indians as active agents and this was an important antidote to the characterisations of them as powerless victims of change that were emerging, especially from the Amazonian context. Studies on ethnic relations in the Amazon region were rather limited at this time – under the influence of Lévi-Straussian structuralism and North American cultural ecology, anthropologists had tended to examine indian social organisation, mythology and symbolism. When ethnic relations were dealt with it was often – not surprisingly under the circumstances – in terms of ethnocide and genocide (Davis, 1977; Jaulin, 1970; but see Barbira-Freedman, 1980) and anthropologists were often advocates for indigenous causes. The plight of Amazonian indians spurred the formation of the campaigning organisation Survival International in 1969.

Seeing indians as active historical agents was therefore important, but some of the difficulties of indians resisting as active agents were also made evident in Isbell's and Whitten's work. The Chuschinos' strategy was to resist by blocking, but in doing so they risked becoming 'a satellite' of the urban migrants' world which, although it was not losing an indian identity in a straightforward manner, was less unequivocally indian (Isbell, 1978: 217). In contrast, the jungle Quichua were actively trying to engage with new economic opportunities, but since their struggle involved intensifying their ethnic identity, they were being blocked by mestizo colonists and constrained by state indian legislation. Thus to be indian and to struggle for progress seemed to be, in Latin American nations, contra-dictory endeavours.

Blacks: Revisionist Histories and Black Culture

Studies of blacks during this period continued to focus on Brazil, although other regions also began to appear, notably Ecuador and Colombia. In many cases, the influence of Marxism, or more broadly, political economy, made itself felt. In contrast to the studies of indians, however, there was less reconsideration of the nature of racial identifications and a continuing tendency to take for granted categories such as black or mulatto, even though the contingent character of these identifications had already been made clear. One of the problems was that, increasingly, observers wanted to emphasise that racism did exist in Brazil and elsewhere and highlighting the flexibility of these categories seemed to work against this trend. The point, in my view, is to reach an understanding of how both flexibility and racism co-exist. The way to grasp this was already implicit in the material on indian–mestizo relations which showed that individuals could move from one category to another, conditional on their move being accepted by others in any given situation, without this abolishing the category indian nor the racism or even the ethnocide directed at that category. However, many of the commentators on race in Brazil were wrapped up in questions of the relation between race and class and this sort of approach escaped them.

Brazil

One example of the concern with race and class was the sociologist Octavio Ianni who, sometimes in collaboration with Fernando Henrique Cardoso, had been writing about race and capitalism in southern Brazil since the 1960s (Cardoso and Ianni, 1960). His approach to this was similar to that of Fernandes in that his predominant concern was with the transition from slavery to capitalism; likewise, his conclusion that white Brazilians adopted 'an ideology of compromise' between allowing social mobility for some blacks and repressing the majority (Ianni, 1966: 51) was similar to Fernandes's notion of 'accommodation'. Ianni took a highly reductionist line, however, arguing that 'the socio-economic and political importance of the labour force clarifies and explains cultural, racial and other manifestations which have been obscured ... by the analyses of some sociologists and anthropologists' (1972: 239). Thus any racial (or ethnic or cultural) identifications and dynamics could be explained in terms of the labour force in a class society; in this view, the position of indians and Polish immigrants is very similar to that of blacks since both are subject to negative stereotypes that facilitate their exploitation as labour (Ianni, 1966: 54–6). There is little hint in any of this that 'black' might be a category worth investigating in its own right: this would be merely the obscurantism of anthropologists.

Historian Carl Degler made an important contribution with his book *Neither Black nor White* (1971), an extended comparison of race relations in Brazil and the US which challenged the idea of racial democracy in the former region. Others such as Toplin (1971) and Skidmore (1972) made similar revisionist interpretations and Toplin also pointed out that, with desegregation and positive discrimination in favour of blacks, the US itself had changed, making the comparison even less straightforward. Degler traced historical differences between Brazil and the US, disavowing the notion of benevolent slavery, but focusing on the so-called 'mulatto escape hatch' which accorded people of mixed ancestry a special place (1971: 107) and allowed them to move up the social scale. This escape hatch, which had emerged for historical reasons connected with the lack of Portuguese women and Portuguese machismo, was the central difference between Brazil and the US.

Degler presented evidence of racial prejudice – much of it anecdotal and impressionistic, but overall quite convincing – and argued that the mulatto escape hatch fitted into a powerful ethos of whitening which held that black was inferior to white, but allowed some upward mobility for individual mulattoes who would then also strive to further whiten themselves by association with non-blacks and by 'marrying up' the racial hierarchy if they could, thus whitening their children even more. This whitening had been noted before by Fernandes and others (for example, Banton 1967) and Skidmore (1974) produced a historical study tracing whitening as an ideology combining ideas of mixture and white superiority and as a government policy on, for example, immigration. Whitening was also part of popular knowledge in Brazil – the adage that 'money whitens' was a well-known one signifying that a wealthy black person might be labelled as non-black and more generally that such a person moved up the racial hierarchy in social terms. Degler simply highlighted the phenomenon of whitening and located its historical roots. The importance of this is that the search for whiteness has to be seen, in my view, as a cultural dimension in its own right; it is, of course, connected strongly to class issues, but it cannot be reduced to them.

Degler also argued that the mulatto escape hatch created 'inner burdens of colour' in the sense that, because there was a possibility of avoiding blackness and successful blacks often did so, many blacks felt ashamed of being black. Furthermore, it was very hard to create the kind of black solidarity movement that the US had witnessed in the 1950s and 1960s, that mobilised blacks as a clear social group and that challenged prevalent negative definitions of blackness. This was also the conclusion of Toplin (1971) and Skidmore (1972). Nevertheless, it should be noted that black activists were already present in Brazil when the UNESCO studies started and they were to become increasingly important (see next chapter). This was something that these analyses, while they recognised the existence of black activists, found hard to cope with, since they assumed that black mobilisation was structurally impeded by the divisions between blacks and mulattoes (and all the other gradations that the whitening syndrome implied). Black activism could never be anything more than marginal in this view.

Winant accuses Degler of class reductionism, saying that his analysis 'saw economic mobility (and thus, integration into a class society) as the key question in Brazilian racial dynamics' (1992: 177), but I find it hard to substantiate this reading. Degler predicts that racism will become more significant and, if anything, makes a plea for greater black solidarity to combat this; he certainly does not tend to 'confirm the traditional wisdom about "whitening" as the preferred solution to Brazil's racial problem' (1992: 177), but rather sees it as part of the problem. My problem with Degler is rather that of an anthropologist with an historian: there is no detailed ethnography showing how racial identifications work in particular situations. He assumes that whitening is mainly a question of special treatment for a mulatto person, allowing him or her (although Degler does not examine the gender issues involved) greater social mobility, but he does not present convincing evidence that this special treatment exists and, in fact, there may be other ways that whitening can occur, such as a black man making money and marrying a lighter woman, or a black woman finding a wealthier white husband or lover (partly due to images of black women as sexually attractive).

Carlos Hasenbalg entered the debate with an argument reminiscent of Bastide's earlier work (which has been too often included with that of Fernandes, but actually departed from it in significant respects). This formed part of what Winant (1992) calls the structuralist approach to race in Brazil and it sought to explain 'the perpetuation of racial inequalities in Brazil' (Hasenbalg, 1985: 27; see also Hasenbalg, 1979). Like Bastide, Hasenbalg argued that racism was not an anachronistic hangover from slavery, but was an active part of capitalist society, working in favour of whites in a competitive situation; 'race as a socially elaborated attribute may be conceptualised as related mainly to the subordinate aspect of the reproduction of social classes' (1985: 27). Here is the class reductionism that Winant claims to find in Degler's approach. However, in maintaining racial inequalities, 'the racist practices of the racially dominant group' included not only actual discriminatory behaviour, but also 'a racist social organisation that restrains the motivation and level of aspiration of non-white people' (1985: 27–8). This, then, brought a level of cultural ideology into the argument that grasped aspects of the ideology and practice of whitening; still, it was subordinated to the reproduction of a capitalist class structure.

Winant adds that both Hasenbalg and Anani Dzidzienyo focused on the 'smooth preservation of racial inequalities' – the subtitle of Hasenbalg's doctoral thesis – or the fact that the 'official Brazilian ideology of non-discrimination ... achieves *without tension* the same results as do overtly racist societies' (Dzidzienyo, 1979: 7) and argues that this conclusion came at a time when Brazil's military regime had crushed most opposition (Winant, 1992: 180–2). In fact, as Winant goes on to argue, and as Andrews (1991, 1992) has also shown in detail, black opposition to racial inequality has a long, if uneven, history. But if Hasenbalg and Dzidzienyo overstated their case (as did Toplin and Skidmore in this respect), they were highlighting what Fernandes had called the 'accommodation' that was characteristic of the Brazilian racial order and that defused some of the tension that racial inequality generated.

Hasenbalg made a further point that contested Degler's central argument about the mulatto escape hatch. His main purpose was to supply hard data showing the degree of racial inequality in Brazil. To this end he analysed 1976 national household survey data and showed, for example, that in terms of occupation blacks and mulattoes got less return for a given level of education than whites did (1985: 38); rates of social mobility were higher for whites than non-whites. This was vital evidence, because much of the argument for the existence of racial discrimination had previously relied on showing that most blacks were in the lower strata (which was liable to be explained away by saying that slavery had put them there and class mechanisms maintained their place) and on anecdotes about exclusion of blacks in specific instances. Here then was irrefutable statistical evidence that blacks and mulattoes were being systematically discriminated against. What was interesting was that Hasenbalg found it logical to compare non-whites to whites; the 'favourable' position of the mulatto seemed irrelevant.

Nelson do Valle Silva, working with the same data base in the 1970s, argued this even more forcefully: he found that mulattoes were discriminated against more than blacks and he specifically rejected Degler's thesis (Silva, 1985). This constituted a challenge to the idea that whitening was a central feature of the Brazilian racial order, but in my view it was misplaced. It obeyed, to some extent, a political desire to combat the force of whitening as an ideology that divided non-whites; it implied that there was an objective basis to the political solidarity of blacks and mulattoes that black activists were trying to achieve. But it therefore under-played the continuing importance of that ideology and, more important, its structural consequences in the society.

For example, both Hasenbalg and Silva ignored the situational nature of racial categorisation and took the survey categories of white (*branco*), mulatto (*pardo*) and black (*preto*) for granted. These were self-identifications in the survey and thus reflect how individuals categorised themselves. However, racial discrimination is about how other people categorise an individual. Silva showed that people who classified themselves as *pardo* suffered more discrimination than those who classified themselves as *preto*. But it is very likely that those who classify themselves as *branco*, who are presumably practising the discrimination, would ascribe the term *preto* to many who claim to be *pardo*. Solaún and Kronus (1973), for example, had demonstrated the tendency of 'whites' in Colombia to 'blacken' the population at large by calling more people 'black' than called themselves 'black'. It is also well known that in Brazil there has been a steady trend of 'whitening' in the censuses with the *preto* category declining and the *pardo* category growing – this may be due to real changes, but it is quite likely due to people re-classifying themselves (Winant, 1992: 179).

In any event, even assuming Silva was right that mulattoes are discriminated against more, both Hasenbalg and Silva showed that mulattoes were still intermediate between blacks and whites; to them the black–mulatto difference was small enough to justify

its analytical removal, but the fact remained and needed explanation. The error was to assume that racial discrimination is the
only factor determining social mobility. The intermediacy of the
mulattoes is not necessarily due to their receiving favourable
treatment. In a system of accommodation, some black people
make money; if they marry white people then their children may
be classified as mulattoes; these children will then have the
benefit of a good education and so on. It may then be the case
that they suffer discrimination and may not get as much return
on their education as a white person, but they are already economically intermediate. The point is that there are structural
links between vertical mobility and whitening which create a general association between being 'whiter' and having more money,
education and power.

Colombia and Ecuador

During this same period, some rather different approaches were
being taken in other regions. Norman Whitten had begun his
research in the town of San Lorenzo, on the Pacific coast of
Ecuador, where the main complex of ethnic and racial identifications involved local blacks and incoming mestizos from the highlands who were exploiting local resources, especially timber. To
do so they had to make use of local black labour and some
blacks, especially lighter-coloured ones, acted as intermediaries in
this situation. Whitten took a Weberian approach to stratification
that did not assume the primacy of class. Instead he looked at
the intersection of class, ethnicity, status (defined as positive
orientation towards the community) and kinship as principles of
social differentiation and concluded that 'ethnic and status lines
divide classes in San Lorenzo; they influence the manner of
participation in the economic order and figure prominently in the
dynamics of social mobility' (1965: 89). Although the mestizos
often looked down on the blacks, they also had to adapt to the
local scene and, although whites and mestizos were at the top of
the class structure, there was a significant black middle class and
blacks in general were taking increasing advantage of the expanding opportunities around them (1965: 202).

Whitten's later book, *Black Frontiersmen* (1974), incorporating
changes since his first study and encompassing the 'wet littoral'
of the Pacific coast from northern Ecuador up into southern
Colombia, was more definitive about the existence of racial

discrimination. The book dealt primarily with black culture in the area, looking at how local blacks adapted to an 'economically marginal' niche which went through boom and bust cycles of natural resource exploitation which also altered the 'social demography' of the zone as outsiders came and went (1986: 4). In terms of local ethnic relations, increasing mestizo immigration had resulted in black disenfranchisement (just as it had for jungle Quichua). Black and mulatto entrepreneurs and intermediaries were being tagged as 'communists' (because of their control over black labour networks), allowing immigrants to take over the best brokerage positions, and immigrants were being more exclusive in their social relations. The Catholic Church was restricting the polygyny which had been a crucial feature in black upward mobility strategies by allowing certain families to accumulate resources. Black women were becoming more autonomous family nodes and, since they were being employed directly in shellfish gathering by whites and mestizos, were less able to participate in black men's upward mobility strategies (1986: ch. 8).

Whitten outlined the idea, which he and others were later to develop, that in Ecuador the overall ideology of the nation as mixed served to exclude blacks (and indians). In practice, 'if access to new resources for those classed as "negro" and "indio" in modernising Latin American nations is blocked, then there is no reason for denying that processes of discrimination leading to *de facto* segregation are under way in the wet littoral and elsewhere' (1986: 198). Here, having done fieldwork in San Lorenzo and among the jungle Quichua, Whitten was taking a broad view of indians and blacks in the nation-state which made a refreshing change from the usual academic separation of these two categories. He also dealt a blow to Harris's idea about the maximisation of ambiguity in racial classification: 'regardless of the various permutations and combinations occurring in racial calculations ... blackness is the opposite of whiteness and national concepts of "mixed" in Colombia and Ecuador stand opposed to "black" just as white is the opposite of black' (1986: 199). This approach was uncompromising about the existence of racism and thus fitted in with some of the statements coming out of Brazil at the same time. It contrasted with the much more benign view of race put forward by Solaún and Kronus (1973) in their study of Cartagena, Colombia, which held that the 'miscegenation-tolerance syndrome' was a dominant trend and would abolish remaining practices of discrimination. Some people, at least, still purveyed the myth of a (potential) Latin American 'racial democracy'.

Whitten also did some collaborative work with the Colombian scholar Nina de Friedemann (Whitten and Friedemann, 1974) who had also been working on aspects of black culture in the Colombian Pacific coastal region. Apart from her interest in kinship structures among blacks in this gold mining region, Friedemann, who is a central figure in the study of blacks in Colombia, was mainly concerned with what she called the 'invisibility' of blacks in Colombian history (except as slaves), in Colombian anthropology and sociology, and in representations of Colombia as a country. Her concern was to expose this racism and to reinstate blacks and their African heritage as a legitimate part of the nation and of academic study (Friedemann, 1984; Friedemann and Arocha, 1986; see also Arocha, 1992). I will return to the overall approaches of Whitten and Friedemann in the next chapter, when I discuss more recent ways of locating indians and blacks in the nation-state.

Michael Taussig's early work fitted in some ways into debates about race and class in the sense that he was concerned with blacks as peasant farmers, under pressure from capitalist expansion and his approach was strongly influenced by Marxism (Taussig, 1980). But he was primarily concerned with issues of cultural resistance and with the devil mythology of black peasants in the Valle region of Colombia, according to which a sugar plantation worker could make a pact with the devil to increase his income, but could only make barren money that had to be squandered in luxury consumption and could not be made productive; meanwhile, the worker's body would waste away. This Taussig interpreted as a judgement, from the perspective of people living in a pre-capitalist mode of production, on the alienating nature of capitalist social relations. The particular concern with the devil was connected by Taussig to the history of slave religion – although it was more generally related to the imposition of Christianity in a colonial regime – and the attempts by blacks to construct their own religious domain, resignifying central elements of Christian symbolism, such as the devil.

Taussig's work thus fitted into the concerns with resistance that I discussed in the previous section, but his angle on this is quite subtle and the kind of defensiveness that Isbell documented is less evident. Peasants' opposition to capitalism is ambivalent: the very myth of the devil pact recognises the desire for luxury capitalist commodities and it hardly constitutes a political strategy. But Taussig asserts that their world view, as expressed in the myth of the devil pact, 'may even simulate the political action necessary to thwart or transcend [the process of commodity formation]' (1980: 17). There is a danger, however, that Taussig is being over-romantic in his depiction of a pre-capitalist mode of production and in his view that the beliefs he documents could stimulate effective political action against capitalism. It remains unclear, moreover, at what point the peasants' opposition to capitalism shades off into a frustrated desire for its commodities.

Black culture

The work of Whitten, Friedemann and Taussig raised the issue of black culture which had been sorely neglected in the Brazilian studies of race and class, with the exception of Bastide's study of Afro-Brazilian religion, first published in 1960 (Bastide, 1978). Indian culture had, of course, long been a legitimate object of attention – even if it turned out to be not that different from mestizo culture – because indians were a legitimate Other in the anthropological gaze. Blacks, in contrast, tended to be seen in cultural terms as ordinary citizens, if second-class ones in economic and political terms. This was least so in Brazil where, for example, Afro-Brazilian religious practice was clearly African influenced and thus evidently 'different' in cultural terms. In Colombia and elsewhere, however, blacks were rarely thought to have a culture *sui generis*.

This is partly why the study of blacks was generally institutionalised as the study of race – with difference signalled by physical features – while the study of indians was that of ethnicity – with the difference signalled by cultural features. This is also partly why, as noted in the previous chapter in relation to the UNESCO studies, blacks tended to be studied in their relations with others, while many studies of indians examined them as cultures in their own right. However, it is clear that cultural features were also important in constituting differences perceived as racial: stereotypes of blacks all over Latin America commonly included ideas about their supposed laziness, happy-go-lucky attitudes, disorganised family life, taste for music and dance and so on. Even if some of these supposed attributes (sexuality, musicality) were seen as natural, it is clear that images of blacks involved a whole way of life, not just a set of phenotypical features. Hence it is important to include the study of black culture in the study of 'race relations'.

Black culture had been studied from very early on – by Ortiz and Nina Rodrigues, for example – but their concerns were not with ethnic or racial identities. Melville Herskovits – who actually started off doing anthropometric studies of blacks in the US as a student of Franz Boas – took up this kind of study in the 1930s, minus the racist trappings. His main interest was in locating African survivals in the New World, although this also involved detailed ethnographic work on many aspects of black culture in Haiti, Brazil and the US (Herskovits, 1966). African survivals and adaptations was a concern that also informed Bastide's work to some extent (Bastide, 1971) and in general set the agenda for the study of black culture in the Americas.

On the question of African survivals, a useful point of departure is that adopted by Mintz and Price (1976) which held that Africans brought to the New World probably shared some basic cultural principles or orientations that underlay the great variety of languages and cultures from which they came.[2] Thus the importance of music and dance in ritual activity was something that a variety of Africans might have had in common and that might have affected how they built up new cultural practices in a slave regime.

But this hardly resolves the heated debates about 'the black family', for example. Many scholars had noted patterns of flexibility in family organisation among blacks all over the Americas – although it was often seen pejoratively as disorganisation, since, for example, cohabitation rather than marriage was often a feature, leading to 'illegitimate' children. Some people saw in this the persistence of some features of African marriage and kinship – for example, the importance of extended families and wide kin networks – others saw it as adaptation to slavery or more generally economic marginality, especially since the same trends could be observed among non-blacks living long-term in similar conditions (see Bastide, 1971; MacDonald and MacDonald, 1978; Whitten and Szwed, 1970: 43). Undoubtedly, whatever patterns existed in the twentieth century were the result of multiple factors, but the debates concerned the exact weighting of these and this was almost impossible to resolve.

The point is that the matter of African survivals was also a question of the construction of black culture in the Americas and this was far from being a simply academic question, but one related to racial identities. Was black culture just an amalgam of European and perhaps Amerindian cultures? Was it something that emerged more or less from scratch in the New World? Did it have significant African roots which would give blacks their own cultural identity? While *candomblé* religious practices in Bahía are clearly African derived, there are no simple answers to these questions at a broader level, partly because they are so emotionally and politically charged and partly because they are very hard to assess with historical evidence – what appears to be of African origin can turn out to be European and vice versa.

Thus black culture became something of a political football all over the Americas, with its status undecided, but important to the growing politicisation of racial identities in Latin America (following the US pattern to some extent). In some areas, black culture appeared to be simply peasant or working class culture, in others it was clearly particular. For some, black culture did not really exist; for others, it was the basis for black consciousness.

Conclusion

The approaches examined in this chapter represented a useful advance on those of the previous decades. Many of them, in the end, despite specific efforts on the part of anthropologists and sociologists to avoid this, remained constrained by a dependency approach and by the limits of debates about the relative roles of ethnicity (or race) and class. Dependency – and more generally a Marxist analysis – were vital in getting a broad view of economic and political inequalities. They also forcefully raised the possibility of locating the social scientist as a political agent. Anthropologists had sometimes acted as advocates for 'their people' in the past, whether to defend them against charges of irrationality, savagery and backwardness or to help them against specific threats to their land and livelihood. A Marxist-oriented perspective grounded this advocacy in a powerful critique of encroaching capitalism and political inequality.

But these approaches could not account for particularities. As Bourricaud (1975: 357) said, the simple fact of Peru's dependency could not help us understand the intricacies of its social stratification system. Such analysis tended to adopt too instrumentalist a view of ethnicity, in which ethnic and racial identities became the expression of economic determinants – even if van den Berghe (1975) assured his readers that he made no *a priori* judgement about the primacy of class over ethnicity. Of course, ethnic and racial identities can hardly be independent of economic concerns, but they can become ends and priorities in their own right alongside those concerns. The business of trying to decide which carries most weight, class or ethnicity/race, becomes then a rather fruitless exercise, trapped within a basically Marxist problematic. The emergence in the 1970s of gender as a major area of debate in the social sciences reinforces this critique – although for a while gender was simply added to the balancing exercises which then juggled three dimensions of difference instead of two. In the end, though, it is not really necessary to assign primacy, but rather to look at how race, ethnicity, class and gender (not to mention age) interact in specific circumstances. The approaches being worked out by scholars such as Whitten and Taussig, while they drew on Marxism and concepts developed in the analysis of colonialism, were moving beyond these towards a perspective that located indians and blacks in the nation-state seen as a political economy *and* a cultural space, itself situated in a global world.

5. BLACKS AND INDIANS IN THE POSTMODERN NATION-STATE

During the 1980s and 1990s, the overall context for understanding race and ethnicity was the analysis of postmodernism. Postmodernism is many different things, but I think it is useful roughly to distinguish between postmodernism as a trend in philosophy and social theory, and postmodernity as a trend in social formations – it goes without saying that the two are linked in complex ways.[1]

Postmodernism is, in part, the paradoxical result of the rational search for certainty. The more systematic this search becomes, the more it reveals that certainty itself cannot be achieved. Of course, relativism is hardly a new epistemological position, but it has received new impetus in this period. In philosophy, deconstructionists such as Jacques Derrida argued that any identity is constructed in relation to difference. There is no solid pre-given centre or simple presence; these exist only in relation to something else (a position that Barth had argued for ethnic groups); therefore, the closure or completion of identification is permanently deferred by differentiation. There is no final reading of a text – and 'text' here has become extended to refer to symbolism in general. Deconstruction, in the broadest sense, thus consists of discovering how certain readings depend on hidden identifications or categories which, when looked at anew, cannot be taken for granted.

Michel Foucault argued that 'discourses' – roughly, modes of representation – construct social realities. People's ways of thinking the world, themselves and others around them are constituted – rather than simply constrained – by discursive formations, that is, more or less coherent ways of representation of a give realm of activity and experience. Thus, for example, the discourse of psychiatry defined certain possible ways of thinking about madness. This is not a question of an external and possibly false 'ideology' influencing people's thought and behaviour; people reproduce the discourse as truth through their own thought and behaviour. It is possible to step outside given discursive formations – this was what Foucault was doing in his historical analysis of them – but it takes a critical effort and, in any case, one cannot step outside discourse itself.[2] Both Derrida and Foucault were part of a so-called 'linguistic turn' in social theory (Giddens, 1987: ch. 4) which involved focusing on language and, more broadly, representation and symbolism.

Lyotard specifically criticised the major 'metanarratives' of Western thought, the grand teleological accounts of the progress of humanity that produce totalising explanations, that is, that seek to explain everything within the compass of one overarching schema. When science seeks after truth, it needs to legitimate its own rules and it achieves this by reference to metanarratives which, according to Lyotard, included the creation of wealth (modernisation), the emancipation of the working subject (Marxism) and of the rational subject. For Lyotard, these metanarratives were questionable and could no longer reign supreme.

Finally, alongside these challenges to the 'Enlightenment project' of rational progress towards systematic, solid knowledge based on science, there was a challenge to the assumed authority of the (mainly Western and mainly male) intelligentsia and scientific community that – the Romantics and doubters such as Nietzsche aside – had carried forward this project. This challenge came from feminism and from postcolonial writers. Feminism raised the possibility of the scientific project as a specifically male project (Merchant, 1983), suggesting that knowledge was not absolute but gendered. From the perspective of the (postcolonised) periphery, postcolonial writers challenged the authority of knowledge produced from (postcolonial) centre. Edward Said (1985), for example, dissected the discursive formation of Orientalism, showing how the East had been constructed as Other in the Western mind by a tradition of representation and how this had affected the production of knowledge about the East.

Ideas of this kind have had several consequences in thinking about race and ethnicity. First, the constructedness of identity has become even more important; feminism has been a crucial influence here. Identity is seen as constructed through complex processes of relationality and representation; it is a process, not a thing, and is constantly under renegotiation (even if the outcome of the negotiation is repeatedly the same for particular individuals).

81

Second, as mentioned in Chapter 1, the reification and essentialisa-tion of identity has been challenged more intensively – the idea is no longer acceptable that a given person or group might have a basic identity that could be characterised in terms of a core, defin-ing essence; groups and indeed individuals are 'decentred', they have no single identity (Hall, 1992a; Landry and MacLean, 1993: ch. 7). As Wilson puts it: 'relationality must be present for identity to exist, but the very basis of meaning in difference leads to the crossing-over of signifiers and the undermining of any pretensions to boundedness' (1995b: 6). Third, multᵢˡ le identities and the chal-lenge to metanarratives both imply that the seemingly 'big question' of the primacy of race/ethnicity *versus* class has become less of an issue. Fourth, culture, or more accurately, the politics of culture, became a central focus. Anthropologists at least had always been concerned with culture – although, as we have seen, the infrastruc-ture of economic relations did preoccupy even them during the 1970s – but now culture was not something that groups just 'had', it was a discursive construct that was lived, but was also open to different readings.

Turning now to postmodernity as a social condition of the late twentieth century, this has been characterised by increasing globalisation as the infrastructure of capitalism has penetrated more pervasively and 'shrunk' the surface of the globe with com-munications technology. It also involves the flexibilisation of capitalism, with globally distributed fragments of production processes being rapidly tailored to volatile market demands. Culture has become increasingly commoditised and culture – whether of the nostalgic past, the present or the future, or of Africa, Asia, the Americas or Europe – is packaged and sold to specific market niches who define their lifestyles by highly differen-tiated consumption – if they can afford to consume at all. Politi-cally, there has been a blurring of class boundaries, the demise of organised working-class politics and the emergence of political mobilisation around a host of issues such as sexuality and gender, ecology, animal rights, housing and other forms of consumption. Nevertheless, some Marxist scholars interpret this as the product of capitalism in its 'late' phase (Harvey, 1989; Jameson, 1991).

This is crucial in the study of race and ethnicity, because of the importance of the social movements that have increasingly emerged around issues of ethnic and racial identity, in Latin America and elsewhere. Related in part to the demise of working-class politics, itself connected to the flexibilisation of capitalism and to the critique of metanarratives, this also fits in with postcolonial critiques which have opened up an intellectual space for the voices of previously marginalised minorities. In Latin America, especially, postcolonial critiques have a long history – Freyre's definition of Brazil as a mixed country and the better for it was, in effect, a challenge to the knowledge about race and modernity produced in Europe and North America – but this was mainly intellectuals speaking on behalf of their nations and perhaps of indians and blacks. Recently, blacks and indians have increasingly been speaking for themselves. The emergence of a politics of culture, mentioned above, is also relevant here, as minority groups give their own readings of their cultures and there are struggles to define the constitution of cultural 'spaces'.[3]

In a globalising world, these spaces are not just local, but national and international: the arena for the constitution of identity is now recognised to be, and indeed to have been for centuries, a global one.

In the rest of this chapter, I will look first at attempts theoretically to locate black and indian cultures in the nation-state and, in the next chapter, at the social movements that have grown around race and ethnicity. My treatment of blacks and indians together in this chapter, as opposed to separately as in previous chapters, partly obeys a minor tendency to do so in the literature, but is more a reflection of my own view that such a synthesis, or at least juxtaposition, is necessary.

Blacks and Indians in the Nation

Within the overall context sketched above, there has been a move towards locating both blacks and indians more firmly within the nation-state. This was not a new concern in itself. The *indigenismo* of the 1920s and the concerns with racial whitening of the same period were all about how to integrate what were seen as problematic or exotic black and indian populations into the modernising nation; but this was about how to define particular nations, rather than analysing the nation or nationalism as such. Considerations of race and class in Brazil were also about the integration of blacks into a class society; this, however, took the nation for granted. A new angle emerged that can be summed up with Benedict Anderson's widely cited definition of the nation as an 'imagined community' (1983). This focused attention on the nation in its cultural and symbolic dimensions and opened the way to asking how blacks and indians as categories imagined by different sets of people might fit into their 'image' of the nation. There is, of course, a danger here that concrete social relations get lost – never Anderson's intention in his analysis of nationalism – but this sort of perspective moved away from the preoccupation with race/ethnicity and class of previous decades towards a greater concern with the nation and with black and indian groups as participating in a space where a politics of cultural struggle was in process.

Mestizaje, whitening and nationalism

Norman Whitten had already shifted his focus of research from blacks on the Pacific coast of Ecuador to indians in the jungles east of the Andes. But a concern with blacks was still present in his writings and this obeyed an attempt to grasp the Ecuadorian nation as a whole in its ethnic make-up. In his 1980s' work, he argues that Ecuadorian nationalism is based on 'an ideology of ethnic homogenization' or 'racial mixture', that is, *mestizaje* (1981b: 15; see also Whitten 1985: 39–44, 223–41; Stutzman, 1981). This ideology can be used to exclude those considered unmixed, the more so because the ideology has 'a tacit qualifying clause which ups the price of admission [to the mixed nation] from mere "phenotypical mixture" to cultural *blanqueamiento* ("whitening", in terms of becoming more urban, more Christian, more civilised; less rural, less black, less indian)' (1981b: 15). People labelled as black and indian – using a variety of possible terms – are most apparent in peripheral areas where natural resources desired by the state and foreign nations are located. Mixed Ecuadorians, who view themselves as true nationals, consider progress to consist in transforming the peripheries of the nation through development that changes both the land and the people on it in ways that conform to 'the ideology and designs of North American industrial growth' (1981b: 14), but are at odds with the ecology of the tropical forest and its management by local people.

Local blacks and indians may resist, either through explicit protest or through 'ceremonial enactment and symbolism' (1981b: 15), making use, for example, of elements of local mythology. The contradictory effect is that blacks and indians in these areas seem to be both 'assimilating to modern Ecuadorian ways, and ... developing into a militant ethnic bloc' (1985: 19); Ecuador itself 'seems to be nationalizing and becoming more diverse at the same time' (1981b:

15). Meanwhile, local *runa* (indigenous people) in the jungles at the borders of the Andes and Amazonia contend with the contradiction between two apparently reasonable principles: 'they are *of* urban Ecuador, and ... they are *of* Amazonia' (1985: 252): they seek a measure of control and autonomy in both systems. There is much in Whitten's approach here that is similar to his earlier work (1986 [1974], 1976), but the presence of the nation-state as a cultural space is now more forceful. This is partly because, by 1981, the indigenous movement had grown in Ecuador to the extent that indianness was a concern at the highest levels of the state, not just as a 'problem', but as a political contender.

Whitten's work has been an important inspiration for my own work on Colombia. The basic ideas about *mestizaje* and *blanqueamiento* that he and Stutzman (1981) elaborated are very similar to the Colombian situation (Wade, 1993a). There seem to me, however, to be certain problems with applying Whitten's ideas directly to Colombia. This is partly because, while there are important populations of black people in the remote and underdeveloped Pacific coastal region, there are also blacks in many other areas of Colombia, including its cities. Whitten's primary focus on blacks (and indians) in peripheral areas led him to see both categories as being stereotypically opposed to the nation; mixed people, and especially developers, classed them as 'non-nationals' (1985: 42). For Colombia, while it is true that in certain planning and academic circles, Pacific coast blacks might be contrasted to *la sociedad nacional* (national society) – with all the overtones of internal colonialism that this invokes – it seems to me that the specificity of the position of blacks in Colombia, and I think elsewhere in Latin America, lies in the fact that they can be classed as both nationals *and* non-nationals. In my view, the location of blacks and indians in the cultural space of the nation-state needs more, and more historical, analysis than Whitten gives it. As I argued in Chapter 2, black identity has never been as institutionalised as indian identity and blacks have been seen much more as (second-class) citizens, typically studied in relation to non-blacks in a 'class society' and often assumed not to have a 'black culture'. In this sense, they have been seen – and, in Colombia, emphatically consider themselves – as nationals. On the other hand, they are also subject to exclusion when whites and mestizos define them as beyond the bounds of legitimate nationality, as non-nationals, as distant from the core values of being (light-coloured) mestizo or white, urban(e), civilised and educated. The sliding between being included by non-blacks ('we

are all brothers, we are all mestizos') and being excluded by them
('blacks are all animals'; 'a monkey dressed in silk is still a
monkey') defines for blacks in the nation a particular space
where they both appear and disappear.

I have also been interested in exploring *blanqueamiento* not
just as an ideology, but as a social practice through which the
hierarchised racial order of Colombia is recreated. The work on
whitening discussed in previous chapters by scholars such as
Degler and Skidmore needs to be complemented by ethnographic
studies of how it works at a grass-roots level and how this level
links to broader ideologies and practices. Looking at blacks and
non-blacks in a small frontier town and in the city of Medellín
(Wade, 1993a), I argued that there are powerful structural links
between non-blackness and upward mobility (see also Martinez-
Alier, 1989). Successful blacks, even when success is by very
local standards, end up being dependent on and/or associating
with non-blacks. Often, even if they have no personal motive to
whiten themselves or their children, they are absorbed into a
non-black social matrix, thus reiterating the hierarchies of the
racial order. On the other hand, non-blacks continue to control
most economic opportunities and blacks who are not successful
are marginalised and depend heavily on family networks to sur-
vive, forming cultural and physical nuclei of blackness which,
again, seem to reiterate national hierarchies by associating blackness with poverty and working-class or rural black culture. For
example, in the frontier town, a handful of blacks were relatively
successful and most of them were linked in significant ways to
non-blacks; some left the town and studied in the capital, Bogotá.
As economic opportunities were increasingly controlled and
expanded by non-blacks in the area, many blacks moved away to
more clearly black, and poorer, parts of the Pacific coast region.
The links of whiteness with success and blackness with poverty
were recreated. In sum, there is a balance between non-black
exclusion and inclusion which is matched by a balance between
black nucleation and dispersal. This is not unrelated to
Fernandes's idea of a system of 'accommodation', but it is vital to
understand this on the level of the cultural space of the nation,
not just the social relations of a class society.

A different way of capturing the notion of accommodation
that addresses its cultural dimensions is the idea of a 'transform-
ist hegemony' elaborated by Brackette Williams, working outside
Latin America, but in a context that is similar in some respects.
In her research on Guyana, she argues that cultural struggles

exist over the value of historical and cultural contributions made by Africans, East Indians, Amerindians and Europeans to the emerging nation, with different groups ranking contributions in different ways (1991: 166). Nationalist attempts to create cultural unity deal with diversity 'by assimilating elements of that heterogeneity through appropriations that devalue them or that deny the source of their contribution'. This constitutes a trans-formist hegemony – a term derived from Gramsci – in which domination works partly by appropriation and resignification. If low-ranked groups maintain their claim to certain cultural contributions in the amalgam of national culture, these are devalued and these groups are defined as 'not "true" members of the ideologically defined nation'. Those claiming status as the real producers of the core elements of national culture have the ideological power to redefine the meaning of the elements appropriated from marginal groups (1991: 30-1). This is a useful approach to ethnicity and race in the nation-state because it directs attention towards processes of resignification by which particular cultural elements become incorporated (accommodated) into nationalist versions of the national culture as long as their significance is defined within the central value complex of the dominant groups – just as individual blacks may be accommodated on condition that they behave in certain 'acceptable' ways.

Overall, this focus on *mestizaje* within the nation sees whitening as a major mechanism of racism in Latin America. It moves away from the classic opposition between the US and Brazil, which anyway has been the subject of reassessment (Skidmore, 1993; Toplin, 1981), and sees each region as operating a different form of racism. I think that, implicit in the classic contrast and helping to shape it, is an unstated assumption about biology. Racism in the US has often been seen as 'deep' – deeply rooted in the social fabric and based on the 'deep' biology of blood and genotype. The contrast is then made with Latin America, where racism is said to be superficial – subordinate to class and based on mere phenotype, only 'skin-deep'. This, in my view, attempts to legitimate the contrast in terms of a mistaken biology – after all, both genotype and phenotype are equally 'biological'. The surface/depth metaphor is misleading, both for biology and for society. There are, of course, real differences between racism in Latin America and the US, but these are historical and cultural, not biological; neither are they helpfully understood in terms of surface *versus* depth (Wade, 1993b).

Ethnohistory and the Nation

Alongside the interest in the nation-state came a concern with history. This had been an integral part of the work of the previous decade, since Marxism and dependency perspectives were very alive to historical change, but the emphasis tended now to be more on history from the native point of view (for example, Harris, 1995a; Hill, 1988; Hugh-Jones, 1989). Some of this work focused on the Andes (see Rivera Cusicanqui, 1993) and not all of it has dealt with locating indians in the emerging nation-state.[4] Harris (1995b), for example, takes a long-term perspective on how indian and mestizo identities have been related to participation in the market, with indian identity today being defined fundamentally by participation in collective institutions (cf. Isbell, 1978), while market activities are more individual. The nation-state hovers in the background, since it constrains the operation of the market, but it is not a central focus.

Tristan Platt (1995), however, tackles markets in the context of nation-building. He argues that it is misguided to see indigenous communities in nineteenth-century (and indeed present-day) Bolivia as resisting the national market and only participating in it through force. While this may have happened, he contends that 'intervention in the market could represent an *Indian strategy*' (1995: 260). Resistance is thus not always as obvious as it might appear. In national debates about the pros and cons of protectionist and laissez-faire trade policies, Platt argues that indians were generally on the side of protectionism and that they struggled to retain colonial-type tributary systems against the republican liberalism that was striving to construct a new nation; in addition, Inca revivalist movements used the symbols of republican nationalism (1995: 287). This is a much more nuanced vision of an ethnic minority in the nation-state than that which sees it simply as an oppressed, victimised minority or assumes the automatic 'resistance' of pre-capitalist economic activity to capitalism.

Platt (1993) argues that nineteenth-century indians in Bolivia had their own 'national projects' involving a 'just' social order for them in economic terms and that they arrived at 'a religious interpretation of the panoply of new invented traditions emerging in coins and public monuments, in heraldry, flags and civic festivals, from the creole architects of the new *Patria*' (1993: 168). For example, in their nationalist imagery, the creoles represented the indians as a young woman being saved from the jaws of the

Spanish by the liberating heroes, paternalist defenders and patri-archal possessors of the nation and her indians. The actual indians were not so helpless and creoles saw them as backward, recalcitrant and savage, to be controlled through the possession (and rape) that was already suggested by the 'saving' of the indian virgin. For the indians themselves, the Virgin Mary was associated with *pachamama*, the earth-mother, while Simón Bolívar, the Liberator, became her son, a Christ-like figure; both underwrote the social reproduction of indian life and community within the new republic. Indians and creoles, then, had different ideas of what the new nation would be like and where indians would fit into it: as virgins to be saved and savages to be civi-lised, or as inhabitants of a sacred space of social reproduction and messianic renewal.

In a widely cited analysis, Joanne Rappaport starts from the assumption that 'history is a question of power in the present, and not of detached reflection on the past' (1990: 15). For the Páez indians of the Colombian Andes, historical consciousness 'is founded on a moral link with the past that is operationalised in the interests of achieving political goals in the present' (1990: 9). The Crown and the state have been a constant presence for these indians, against which they have fought to define their autonomy, using both written and oral histories as 'a vehicle for changing the course of history' (1990: 180). The histories themselves are reshaped as changes occur in the political context in which they are articulated and today they work to create a 'textual com-munity' (1990: 183) which acts as a basis for defining the Páez as an ethnic group, based in part on the central role of literate indian leaders who can operate in both directions at the interface of the oral and the literate, but also on the history embedded in the landscape which is readable by everyone. In Rappaport's analysis, then, indian resistance and ethnic identity within the nation-state is built around historical consiousness (see also Rappaport, 1994).

Indians and the Nation-State

Seeing indians in the context of the nation-state from a post-modernist perspective indicates that 'none of the terms ... *Indians*, *nation-states*, and *culture* are monolithic and static cat-egories' (Urban and Sherzer, 1991b: 12). The papers in their collection (Urban and Sherzer, 1991a) demonstrate that indian ethnic identities and the nation-states are highly interdependent and, in some sense, mutually constitutive.[5] Indeed, I think that some of the shift by anthropologists towards seeing indians within the nation-state is due to indians increasingly coming to see themselves as ethnic groups within the nation as a result of their historical experiences (Turner, 1991; Jackson, 1991).

Abercrombie – interestingly, a historian – writing on the K'ulta of the Oruro region of Bolivia, states:

> Modern day 'indigenous ethnic groups' and 'indigenous cos-mologies' are unintelligible apart from their struggle with the state: they are founded upon its existence, and they are recreated only in so far as they can maintain, and mould to their own purposes, a 'state within'. (1991: 111)

In his view, 'the gods of the oppressors ... are required for the reproduction of K'ulta society' (pp. 110–11) in that, for example, the rituals that the K'ulta use to ensure the reproduction of their society identify local ritual leaders with Jesus Christ and invest them with elements of Christian saintly power. In other words, local cosmology has adapted to Christian hegemony which is then necessary for indian society.

Of course, it has been widely recognised that 'indian culture' has for a long time been a hybrid of different elements (Fried-lander, 1975; Harris, 1995b: 359): the point is, however, not to see ethnic identity as something which simply persists despite this, but rather as something that emerges in that interaction. Abercrombie overstates his case, however, in so far as he implies that indigenous ethnic groups are totally dependent on the state for their very existence. In contrast, Howe shows how Kuna indian identity has been formed in long-term *interaction* with the Panamanian state. For a start, part of the identity of the Kuna, who live on a series of islands off the Caribbean coast of Panama, is their dress complex, particularly for women. This complex, however, only appeared in the nineteenth century, since its nose-rings, bead bindings, and the famous Kuna *molas* (hand-stitched appliqué designs worn on wom-en's blouses) were based on imported goods; it also developed partly in response to contact (Howe, 1991: 25). The drinking of *chicha* beer in parties also became an important symbol of Kuna identity, but this was partly because the Panamanian state dis-approved of it and tried to stop the practice in the 1920s during a programme of forced acculturation which also targeted the wearing of leg-bindings by women.

Howe's chapter also shows that there is no simple opposition between the Kuna and the state, in this case the police: some policemen had female Kuna companions, despite the jealous guarding of Kuna women by their menfolk; some Kuna also opposed the *chicha* parties; some of the police were themselves Kuna. Furthermore, Howe demonstrates how other parties come into the interactive constitution of identity. The Kuna attracted attention in the US as possible 'white indians' and there were a number of expeditions to study them. In 1925, the Kuna revolted against the acculturation programme to which they were being subjected and received support from the US, partly because some North Americans saw them as noble indians being crushed by a basically black or mulatto nation-state. Thus identity was being constructed in an international frame.

Jackson's chapter (1991) reaffirms this: an 'ethnic' identity for the Tukanoans of Colombian Amazonia is an emergent phenomenon, in a process that elsewhere has been labelled 'ethnogenesis' (see Hill, 1996, for a recent view). In this case, identity emerges in a complex interaction between government agencies, national indigenous organisations, Protestant missionaries, the Church, anthropologists and different factions within the Tukanoans. The state has adopted different positions in response to indigenous organisation which emerged in Colombia in the 1960s in the Andean regions: it has varied between official repression (for example, under President Turbay, 1978–82) and official recognition (for example, with the 1991 constitution). Indigenous organisations based on Andean indian experience are also active in the Amazon region and their representations of indian society are being adopted by Tukanoan activists: 'Tukanoans are learning how to be proper Indians from non-Tukanoan Indian images and values' (1991: 147). The image of an 'indian community' with its own culture and boundaries is especially inappropriate for the Tukanoans since the practice of language exogamy (marrying someone who speaks a different language from oneself) continuously blurs cultural boundaries, yet this is the image that both highland indigenous organisations and government agencies are used to and it is thus deployed by Tukanoan activists as well. The Catholic Church sponsors the local indigenous organisation because it wants to reassert its authority in an area where North American Protestant evangelical missionaries are active. The Tukanoans themselves divide over 'progress' or 'tradition' and anthropologists also have different agendas depending partly on institutional splits between more 'academic' and more 'applied' orientations (Wade, 1993a: 33–4). The overall result is that Tukanoan 'culture' has become a reified object, subject to representation, negotiation and attempts at preservation – in 1983, for example, the Ministry of Health established a 'shaman school' for older men to teach younger ones (Jackson, 1995).

If indian identity is constituted within the context of the nation-state, the opposite is also true. Howe contends that, in order 'to cast themselves as the forces of order, and state control as the only appropriate kind of order, [the Panamanian authorities] *needed* the Kuna to be anarchic' (1991: 34). To construct its order and civilisation, the nation-state needs disorder and savagery, and these may be seen as internal rather than external. On the other hand, the ideology of *indigenismo* used indians to confer uniqueness to Latin American national identities in a global world (see Chapter 2) and this is still common today. Hendrickson (1991) argues that, in Guatemala, indian *traje* (clothing) is used by government agencies, in tourist information and in beauty contests, as both a symbol of the uniqueness of Guatemala and a symbol of its supposed unity. Meanwhile, indian dress when worn by an indian in daily life is also a mark of low status. Similarly, Abercrombie argues that 'urban "non-Indians" continue to make the relationship of their culture to that of "Indians" fundamental to their own identities' (1991: 96), by defining themselves as that which is not indian. Thus, for example, in the city of Oruro, mestizos hire indian shamans during carnival time to make offerings in an 'indian' way to deities thought to be indian. This constructs indians as ritually powerful, but at the same time as fundamentally different. 'All [the Oruro carnival dance groups] represent, in some form, an "Indian within", elevated to a high and powerful rank within urban "folk" religion, as it is within a nationalism in sore need of an anti-imperialist and legitimating identity' (1991: 119). The nation needs indians to specify a unique identity, non-indians need access to an identity that 'taps the wild powers apparently unattainable for ... civilised folk' (1991: 119).

The Power of Blacks and Indians

To talk of 'wild powers' may seem fanciful – hardly a central element of racial and ethnic distinctions – but Taussig's work indicates that this is far from the case. Focusing on Colombia, where indians are a tiny minority, Taussig says that 'the enormity of the magic attributed to those Indians is striking' (1987: 171);

the more 'savage' and remote the indians, the more powerful they are said to be – even among the indians themselves. The power they are said to control is sought after to solve the classic trilogy of life's problems – *amor, salud y dinero* (love, health and money). Indian curers work in frontier towns, but also advertise in the national newspapers. The hallucinogenic drink, *yagé*, used in ritual curing, comes from the Amazon region, but is also on sale in Bogotá. This attribution of magic, argues Taussig, is 'a cunningly wrought colonial *objet d'art*' in that it stems from ideas about 'wild men' – savage yet powerful – that existed before the conquest of the Americas and were transferred onto indians; it is also, however, 'third world modernism, a neocolonial reworking of primitivism' (1987: 172) in that the spread of capitalism has actually given more power to indians as people feel more distant from the source of 'primitive' strength. Taussig is hardly unaware of the economic factors in the construction of identity, but 'to focus exclusively on the conscious economic interests of the individual is to lose sight of colonial mythopoesis working through the political unconscious' (1987: 185). There are politico-*cultural* dimensions of identity that are missed by the politico-*economic* bias of instrumentalist approaches to ethnic and racial identity.

Blacks in Colombia are also attributed powers as healers and sorcerers – usually those from the isolated Pacific coastal region. In Brazil, African and Afro-Brazilian deities are worshipped and asked for help in *candomblé* and Umbanda religions by all kinds of people; some *candomblé* ritual specialists travel to West Africa and return to their religious centres back in Brazil with 'authentic' and revitalising ritual practices (Henfrey, 1981: 95). Herein, again, lies a long history of the attribution of magical power – dangerous and powerful, evil and enticing – to Africans and their descendants (Taussig, 1987: 217; Wade, 1993a: 293).

With blacks in Latin America (and elsewhere), just as important are the intertwined images of sexual, musical and dancing power. This is an underlying element in the literary trends of *negrismo* that emerged in the 1920s (see Chapter 2), as it is in the phenomenon of sun-tanning that emerged at about the same time. The ambivalent sexual attraction felt by whites for blacks is also a recurrent theme in colonial contexts (Young, 1995). Sex and music often fit together. In Colombia, for example, definitions of national music in the early decades of this century centred on guitar-based styles associated with the white/mestizo Andean interior. By the late 1940s, 'tropical' styles associated with the Caribbean region of the country and with the Caribbean basin itself were all the rage, despite grumpy protests from some conservatives about 'foreign' and even 'African' music swamping 'authentic' Colombian music. The reasons for the rise of this music are complex, but one element was the 'modern', liberated sexuality it was held to embody (Wade, n.d.).[6] Styles of music associated with blacks, or as danced to by blacks, are still seen as sexually immoral and/or exciting by many people in Colombia (Wade, 1993a: 245-52).

This, in itself, is not new. The point is that, within the cultural space of the nation, images of racialised powers – indian magic, black sexuality, white civilisation – are symbols competing for room, for legitimacy, in defining what the nation is and can become. Shamanism has been seen as a vital institution, internal to indian groups, that helps them to endure as cultural units (for example, Elsass, 1992; see also Langdon and Baer, 1992). But shamanism also works interactively in the construction of indian identity as part of a much broader, national and indeed inter-national cultural space. Music can also be important in under-writing black identity in specific locales, but this likewise occurs within a national musical context – and indeed a whole 'black Atlantic' diaspora (Gilroy, 1993a) – of musics identified as more or less black (see Béhague, 1994).

This gives a rather different view of racial and ethnic identi-ties in the nation-state. This has been and still is largely analysed as a struggle over economic resources and political power, but there are important cultural, symbolic and moral dimensions as well. From this perspective, it is even more necessary to see indians, blacks and the nation as mutually constituting cultural categories. To sustain itself, the nation feeds on the power of blacks and indians, just as they feed on the power of the nation-state.

6. BLACK AND INDIAN SOCIAL MOVEMENTS

The national context has become a vital one for understanding ethnic and racial identities, partly because of the emergence of movements that seek to revitalise those identities and make indians and blacks players in the national politics of economy and culture. These movements often feed on symbolic and concrete links with each other and with movements outside Latin America, making the international context important too (Brysk, 1996; Fontaine, 1981).

Black and indian social movements have been around for a long time. Recent ethnohistorical works have highlighted the importance of slave and indian rebellions, runaway slave communities, the contribution of slaves' resistance to abolition and so on.[1] The Frente Negra Brasileira was active in the 1930s (Andrews, 1992), black organisations were around in Brazil when the UNESCO studies were being carried out (Fernandes, 1979: 98) and the Movimento Negro Unificado was formed there in 1978 (González, 1985). In Colombia, black organisations date from the 1970s (Wade, 1995a). Indigenous rights organisations likewise sprang up all over Latin America from about the 1960s.[2] However, it has been in the 1980s and 1990s that these movements seem to have gained strength and multiplied.

'New' Social Movements

The reason why black and indian social movements have attracted more attention recently is partly because of their proliferation, but also because they form part of a more general phenomenon, termed 'new' social movements, although there is debate about how 'new' they really are. They include everything from squatters' associations, Christian Base Communities and animal rights groups to workers' cooperatives, indigenous land rights organisations and ecological groups.

They are said to be new because they seem to be different from the classic trades union workers' protest of earlier decades: there is less of an emphasis on either modernisation or revolution as the basic options, and more on the multiplicity of political spaces that can be carved out in the nation, and the globe, in which 'politics' is no longer a separate level, but is integral to social life. There is also often less emphasis on the sphere of production (labour *versus* capital) and more on 'reproduction' (for example, of the environment, whether urbanised or rural). Among new social movements, a divide has also been identified between 'strategy' and 'identity' – the extent to which a movement focuses on strategic, instrumental ends (for example, obtaining land) or on asserting a right to a cultural space for its identity (Escobar and Alvarez, 1992; Escobar 1992b; Foweraker, 1995). The point is that identity as *an end in itself* constitutes something of a new trend. Hall contends that the decentring of the modern subject and the dislocation of stable foci of identification by globalisation have brought about a new search for identities (Hall, 1991, 1992a). Escobar argues that, for many in Latin America, modernity itself has failed as a project and new forms of grassroots collective action have emerged (Escobar, 1992a). In a similar vein, Kearney writes that 'in this postdevelopment moment [in Latin America] ... conditions that promote diversity appear to be deepening, creating a climate conducive to the resurgence of indigenous identities' (Kearney, 1996: 8).

This forms the overarching context for the emergence of these movements. At a more specific level, other factors intervene. For example, indian organisation has generally been more successful than black organisation, as shown by the example from Colombia given in Chapter 2. This, in my view, is to do with the institutionalisation of indian identity which gave indians a conceptual, political and often a territorial basis – hence the importance of land rights struggles – on which to organise themselves. That identity also helped them gain international backing. Blacks, in contrast, have not had this. Observers such as Toplin (1971), Degler (1971), Skidmore (1972), Hasenbalg (1979) also argued that, whether due specifically to the special place of the mulatto or more generally to a system of accommodation based on whitening, black mobilisation was inherently difficult to achieve. This is still the case to some extent (Burdick, 1992a; Hanchard, 1994; Wade, 1993a: ch. 17), but previous analyses, by treating black mobilisation as blocked by a permanent structural obstacle, find it hard to account for changes in this mobilisation. I think it is more fruitful to relate black political mobilisation to the overall political context, so that in Brazil it flowered with democratic opening and in Colombia with constitutional reform (Arocha, 1992; Wade, 1995a).

Because of the fragmentation of the political scene, one characteristic of black and indian movements is the intertwining of different axes of identification and action: ethnicity, race, gender, class, sexual orientation, religion, music and so on. For example, in Brazil an early if amorphous black movement was the 1960s 'Black Soul' movement which emulated some of the ideology and trappings of the US black power movement and took US black soul music as a focal point. Then in the 1970s, Winant argues that blacks were active in the strengthening of democratic political opposition to military rule, later going on to organise as blacks; class and racial identities were continuously overlapping and intersecting here and, for example, a Black Commission was created within the Partido Trabalhador. Winant also mentions the *afoxés*, groups rooted in Afro-Brazilian religious practice which are active in carnival as dance and musical groups, but which also act as community associations with political and self-help ends (Winant, 1992). Within all these organisations and groups, there is great debate about what weight to give class, race, gender and so on as organising, mobilising principles – should blacks seek to participate in national political structures along class lines, or work against these through socialism, or focus on reaffirming black identity above all else? Should men and women organise separately or together? These questions – which are familiar enough to a European or North American reader – are not easily resolved, but the point is that they indicate the increasing importance of the politics of identity, difference and culture in issues of race and ethnicity in Latin America.

Ethnicity, Race and Class

Class remains a vital concern in the broad sense that most of these movements include a struggle for material goals, often land. In Colombia, black organisations emerged in the 1970s, taking inspiration from the US's Black Power and civil rights movement. The use of North American black symbolism continues, but taken over nowadays by the more recognisably Caribbean and Latin

American imagery of the *cimarrón* (runaway slave) and the *palenque* (runaway slave community), particularly with the national organisation Cimarrón – which continues to be a small affair, compared to the national indigenous organisation. The principal concern here was black identity and consciousness-raising among urban blacks. During the 1980s, the Church formed many 'peasant organisations' (as well as indigenous organisations) in the Pacific coastal area and these were mainly for local blacks. The main concerns were land, farming and infra-structure, but black history and identity were also promoted by Church personnel – some of whom were members of Cimarrón. In the early 1990s, with constitutional reform going on, opening a forum for blacks and indians to voice their concerns, black organisations multiplied and the same sort of debates as in Brazil took place, dividing black groups. Cimarrón began to work with peasant associations, making class issues a more important part of its agenda, but still linking them to issues of black identity (Wade, 1995a).

The importance of land insistently brings class issues into ethnicity for blacks and indians alike. At a very general level, much of the recent history of many Latin American countries has involved attempts to turn 'indians' into 'peasants', with resistance often phrased in more or less ethnic terms (Mallon, 1992). Sendero Luminoso in Peru, although a Maoist organisation, is argued by some to have had certain ethnic character (Varese, 1996: 65; cf. Poole and Renique, 1991). Schryer shows how in the region of Huejutla in central Mexico, 'militant peasants identified with their struggle [over land] in terms of an ethnic conflict between Indians and non-Indians' (1990: 4). Because conflicts over land cut across ethnic boundaries, however, there were divisive disputes among indians about whether to join land invasions and about the meaning and function of central indian cultural institutions such as the civic-religious hierarchy and communal land tenure. In contrast, the Ejército Zapatista de Liberación Nacional in Chiapas, although taking a patriotic line with statements that 'There is in us, as in Our Great Mexican Nation, indigenous and mestizo blood', also clearly has a basically indigenous identity: 'we believe that if thousands of indigenous people rise up in struggle, then it is a matter of indigenous insurrection'. The causes of the rebellion are connected to land, neo-liberal reform, the impact of liberation theology and so on, but also to the racism that indians have for centuries experienced at the hands of local mestizos.[3] Finally, Peter Gose outlines the division in the southern Peruvian Andes between indigenous peasants, who produce directly from the land with collective labour, and mestizos, who use private labour and appropriation. this class division is, however, expressed through Andean cultural categories with participation in collective ritual and adherence to an ideology of egalitarianism being central to indian identity (Gose, 1994).

In the Amazon region, the overlap of land issues – and now guardianship of biodiversity (Varese, 1996) – with indian identity is also fairly clear. In the Colombian and Brazilian Amazonia, for example, indians may legally own land reserves, although their rights are frequently abused by colonists and indeed the state (Treece, 1990; Branford and Glock, 1985). In the Pacific coastal region of Colombia, 1993 legislation gives black rural communities there access to communal land rights in a way which consolidates the existing ethnic division between local blacks and non-black colonists (Wade, 1995a). This, however, does not mean there are no internal divisions within black communities or indian groups – on the contrary, there are intense and sometimes violent disputes within indian 'groups' and reserves in Colombia (Jackson, 1991; Kloosterman, 1996), amongst Miskitos in Nicaragua (Vilas, 1989; Scherrer, 1994), or amongst blacks in Colombia's Pacific coast region.

The juggling of race/ethnicity and class thus goes on in a very practical way in all these regions, as concerns of land and identity overlap and interweave. Scholars analysing the process differ and some retain a basically Marxist approach against what they see as the abandonment of political economy by postmodernists, but even they accord cultural dimensions a good deal of autonomy (Kearney, 1996). Generally, however, the debate is now less about the primacy of race/ethnicity *versus* class and more about how they interact with each other – and with other dimensions of difference. In addition, the emergence of ecological concerns has shifted the balance away from ownership of land (a class issue) towards the reproduction of the environment, although these two aspects cannot be dissociated (Blauert and Guidi, 1992; Collinson, 1996). The demand for land by indians, and indeed the ceding of land to indian communities by the state, often has the explicit aim of 'protecting the environment'. Fisher observes that the Kayapo of the Brazilian Amazon purvey the image of them as resisting the threat of environmental degradation because it is in their 'nature' to do so. In their case, however, this image is manipulated by them in their strategic engagement with the state, and they do not, according to Fisher, have an 'environmental consciousness' as such (Fisher, 1994: 229–30).

Ethnicity, Race and Religion

Given the importance of Afro-Brazilian religion in Brazil, it is not surprising that this has also formed a focus of identification, and not just for the *afoxés*. There is a tremendous variety of religious practice from different types of *candomblé*, involving worship of and possession of the devotee by African deities (who may be symbolically paired with Christian saints), through Umbanda, a more recent and electic religion combining elements of *macumba* (similar to *candomblé*) and European spiritism, to Catholicism and Pentecostalism. There has been a good deal of debate about the political character of different groups and the extent to which they reinforce or challenge the status quo. Brown (1986), for example, argues that Umbanda groups generally reproduce relations of patronage and inequality, but Henfrey (1981) shows how, *within* working-class *candomblé* in Bahía, subtle differences between groups in terms of religious practice and symbolism (conscious African orthodoxy about deities and 'serious' behaviour *versus* a more eclectic attitude to deities and a more 'fun' approach) fit into different class relations (old-style proletariat working in paternalistic relations for white masters who patronise 'African-style' *candomblé versus* new-style proletariat working in factories whose more eclectic religious activities are not controlled by this patronage). Therefore, religious symbolism and practice are open to a wide variety of interpretations and Brown's conclusions may have been largely due to the middle-class focus of her study (see also Ireland, 1992; Rostas and Droogers, 1993).

Thus, while the emergence of Umbanda may have involved the whitening of *macumba*, by removing certain elements seen as African and savage (Brown, 1986), when it is practised in a low-income settlement in Rio, where most people are black and mulatto, it can take on a much 'blacker' and working-class feel. Equally, *afoxés* that have roots in Afro-Brazilian religion may take a radical line on black identity in Brazil, but, as Henfrey argues, the 'serious' (re)-Africanised *candomblé* centres fit rather well into the traditional patronage of the exoticised cultural difference that is seen to encapsulate, in Freyre's words, 'certain values of general interest or artistic importance' (1951: 119) – and indeed they are widely patronised by the middle classes.

In sum, religion intertwines with ethnic and racial identities in unpredictable ways; what is important is that it can be a significant element in their construction. Burdick (1992b), for example, reports that in Rio de Janeiro a Christian Base Community, drawing on liberation theology, had a light-skinned leadership and failed to disturb racism in its midst. In contrast, the Pentecostal Assembly of God, with its discourse of radical personal transformation and the spiritual empowerment of the humble, managed to attract many blacks, some of them in positions of leadership. On the other hand, liberation theology has been important in sponsoring indigenous identity in Chiapas (Renard, 1994), while among the Guatemalan Q'echi', Catholicism provided in the past and still furnishes 'the organisational structure and discursive medium binding communities together in political action' (Wilson, 1995a: 307).

Ethnicity, Race, Gender and Sexuality

Perhaps the most important departure from the race/ethnicity and class theme has been that involving gender. I have only mentioned gender tangentially until now, because only in the 1980s and 1990s has it really become an issue in studies of race and ethnicity in Latin America. It did not occur to, say, van den Berghe to ask whether being male or female made any difference to indian or mestizo identity in 1970s San Jerónimo, even though feminism was flowering in social science at the time. The way that women (although not necessarily gender inequality) did enter debates was mainly through studies of the family, particularly the black family. Women as well as men were also inevitably involved in discussions of race mixture, although it is striking how, for example, Mörner (1967) manages a history of race mixture which ignores the issue of gender inequality.

Martinez-Alier (1989 [1974]) dealt in more detail with the problem, showing that upper-class men could have covert (or even overt informal) relations with women lower down the racial ranking without this threatening their status – even marriage was less dangerous – because their position as men allowed this. White women, in contrast, would dishonour themselves and their families, because their sexuality was seen as a male possession. Thus white dominance was partly effected by white male control over white women, whether they liked it or not. Black and mulatto women could be mediators of social mobility in the sense that, again whether they planned this or it was forced on them, having a sexual relationship with a white(r) man could spell economic advantages for them and any resulting offspring. But the racial difference often meant an informal union which could label the woman, but not the man, as sexually immoral. Bastide (1961) recognised many of the same processes for contemporary Brazil, but he spoke about white men 'defending' white women's honour and thus glossed over gender inequality. Indeed, it was not until Martinez-Alier's preface to the second edition of her book that she wrote: 'In nineteenth-century Cuba the reproduction and reinforcement of class inequality [took place] through the interplay of racial discrimination and gender hierarchy' (1989: xv).

The importance of gender for understanding racial and ethnic identities stemmed from the dissatisfaction of black feminists with, on the one hand, the patriarchal attitudes of black male activists (bell hooks, 1981) and, on the other, with the ethnocentrism of white feminists (Carby, 1982; Amos and Parmar, 1984). Feminism tended to use either a notion of patriarchy that opposed all men to all women as rather homogeneous categories sharing an essential interest, or a political economy approach that focused on the exploitation of women's labour in domestic and work contexts. All in all, existing approaches seemed to ignore that black women might have a particular perspective and position (Anthias and Yuval-Davis, 1992: ch. 4). For example, radical feminism had targeted rape as a male instrument for the oppression of women. But in the US the accusation of raping a white woman had typically prompted the lynching of black men, so its meaning was different for black women. Or again, Marxist-feminist explanations of women's low wages often pointed to the real or supposed dependence of women on men. But black (African-American and African-Caribbean) women in Britain and the US, while they still receive low wages, tend to be less dependent on a male wage than white women. Therefore, it would seem that racial discrimination is creating a specific problem for black women, who may deal with it partly through reciprocity within extended family networks that permits them to continue working full-time despite low wages. The answer to these analytical problems is to avoid reducing varied empirical situations to the determinations of one or two underlying factors (patriarchy, class), and instead to look at the intersection of various factors, assessing their relative roles in specific cases.

Gender has also been an important axis of critical analysis for understanding the nation and colonialism – both of which, as we have seen, are important contexts for race and ethnic identities. According to McClintock, nationalism is 'constituted from the very beginning as a gendered discourse, and cannot be understood without a theory of gender power' (McClintock 1993). Nationalist discourses and practices call on women in various ways: as reproducers of biological offspring which swell the nation's population, as producers of cultural offspring who will know where they belong, as symbols of national boundaries and national identities, as participants in national struggles, and as workers in the national labour market (Anthias and Yuval-Davis, 1992: 115). They may be seen positively in any of these roles, but as Guy shows in her study of prostitution in Argentina, they may also be seen as a threat, polluting the nation with their sexuality (1991).[4]

Gender and sexuality are not the same thing, but since gender difference is often seen in terms of sexual difference and since gender inequality often involves control over sexuality, the two are closely connected – as we have already seen in Martinez-Alier's work on Cuba and as is implied in Guy's work on Argentina. This is perhaps most evident in relation to colonialism and race. As bell hooks says: 'Sexuality has always provided gendered metaphors for colonisation' (1991: 57). Colonisation, whether within or beyond national boundaries, has often been seen as the male domination of feminised space, construed variously as wild, unruly, seductive, submissive, or threatened. In colonial contexts, the boundaries of colonial domination have frequently been sexual boundaries as well, with important material and symbolic dimensions whether or not they were crossed. And crossed they usually were, because as Young says, 'Colonialism ... was not only a machine of war and administration, it was also a desiring machine' (1995: 98) – and the object of desire was the power of black sexuality. Hence, 'Sex is at the very heart of racism' (Hyam, 1990: 203).

All this may seem to be wandering far from away from black and indian social movements, but there are crucial connections. The point is that because gender and sexuality are so integral to the construction of racial and ethnic identities, the movements that form around these identities are inevitably affected by this. Thus, for example, when one female black activist in Colombia was told by a black male colleague that it 'looked bad for a woman in her position' that she was going out with a non-black man, a whole tangled history of sexualised, racialised relations was conjured up. The idea that white men sexually exploited black women under slavery, that some black women had relations with ('sold themselves to') white(r) men to move themselves and their children up the social hierarchy, that black men did not have the same access to this channel of social mobility – all this was invoked in the implicit charge that this particular black woman was betraying her 'race', betraying the racial solidarity that was expected of 'a woman in her position'. Here, to use Gilroy's words, 'racial sameness [was experienced] through particular definitions of gender and sexuality' (1993a: 85).

In a different example, the black social movement in Colombia, and I'm sure elsewhere, has to deal with the fact that black women and black men are located in urban labour markets in ways that are different from each other and from non-black women and men. Black women migrants from the Pacific coastal region to the big cities of Colombia tend to concentrate in domestic service, to a greater extent than non-black migrant women. This is due partly to the stereotype of black women as servants which makes it hard for them to get jobs doing anything else. They can carry on with this work, even after they have children, partly by sending their children back to live in extended family networks in the Pacific coastal region (Wade, 1993a: 186–93). Thus 'black activism' in these cities consists partly of mobilising and defending the particular labour rights of these women. Black social movements are structured by both the gender and sexual aspects of black identity and experience.

For indigenous movements, the issue of sexuality seems to be less important, but gender is still of vital importance. It has been noted that indian women seem to be more 'traditional' than men and this seems to be because they have less contact with the urban or outside world. Marisol de la Cadena (1995) indicates how changing gender hierarchies create this phenomenon. In Chitapampa, near Cuzco, villagers distinguish each other as 'indians' and 'mestizos'. Even though they all seem like indians to people from Cuzco, those who have more experience of urban environments and hold a dominant economic position in the community are 'mestizos'. Most 'indians' are women and this is partly because they have little experience of the type of urban work that helps to define a mestizo. This in turn is because, as land-holding has lost its material and ideological value, women have found themselves inheriting plots of land previously controlled by men who are more interested in commerce and urban work. Women work these plots in order to underwrite men's urban ventures, supplying a rural safety net.

Hence 'household strategies of survival confine women to the ideological sphere of rural Indianness' (1995: 337). Many women do begin to move away from a 'traditional' indian identity in the village, marketing produce in Cuzco, or working as domestic servants, but this work is still seen as inferior to men's work. Although this is only one case, it indicates that if part of the perceived inferiority of indianness is linked in a self-reinforcing cycle to the perceived inferiority of women, then mobilising around indianness will have to address issues of gender inequality at the same time as those of ethnic inequality. This is a challenge that the Zapatistas of Chiapas have taken seriously with a Law on Women's Rights passed within the EZLN in January 1994.[5]

Official Multiculturalism

What has been the outcome of black and indian mobilisations? Some states have reacted to black and indian social movements by passing new legislation – even constitutions – that recognise multiculturality or special rights for ethnic groups: for example, Colombia, Bolivia, Brazil and Nicaragua.[6] There seems to be a certain official acceptance of postmodern celebrations of diversity – what one might call a postmodern nationalism that defines the nation in terms of its multiculturality, rather than an ideally homogeneous culture.

However, such strategies often seem to obey motives of political control, and this indicates that these new trends are still subject to the play of power and resources that were so important to the dependency and Marxist perspectives of the preceding decades. In that sense, postmodernity is not a radical rupture with previous social relations: there are strong continuities with the past.

In the Nicaraguan case, the Sandinista government pledged early on to do away with discrimination against Miskitu and other indian groups and creole blacks, all living in the eastern coastal region. In practice, Miskitu groups wanted some control over local affairs and the Sandinistas resisted this. The upshot was that confrontations became embroiled in the US–Contra–Sandinista war, with Miskitu and other indigenous groups taking up arms against the Sandinistas. By 1987, the Sandinistas had relented and passed the Law on Autonomous Regions of the Atlantic Coast which gave a good deal of local power to various groups there and instituted bilingual and bicultural education programmes. There is no denying that this was ground-breaking in Latin America and represented real progress for creole and indigenous autonomy in the region, but it is also true that the Sandinistas were forced into these concessions by the war and that 'the law expresse[d] mainly the government and FSLN [Sandinista] approach to the question' (Vilas, 1989: 177). Scherrer notes that the way the law was drafted has meant that 'the past four years have shown continuous usurpation of control over eastern Nicaragua's resources and over the budgets of the regional governments by central authorities' (1994: 121–2). The demise of the Sandinistas in 1990 is a large part of the cause of this and Freeland notes of the black creoles that, under the Chamorro government, 'they have been unable to advance either regional or ethnic rights' and that 'responsibility for much of this failure lies with Managua' (Freeland, 1995: 190).

In Colombia, the state has historically been rather weak, especially in peripheral areas of the country. Indian organisation, which began as a 'peasant' struggle for land and became a self-consciously indian one, has been a thorn in the side of the state and landowners since the 1970s. Indians also participated in armed guerrilla insurrection in the form of the Quintín Lamé movement. At different times, the state attempted to repress indians and co-opt them, and as part of the latter tactic, land grants have been made, resulting in the indian population (2 per cent of the censused total) today owning 22 per cent of the country's land surface. In 1991, a new constitution was passed, in the drafting of which indigenous organisations played a significant role, even though reform was more part of the demobilisation of (non-indian) guerrilla groups than co-opting indian groups. The constitution gave important land and cultural rights to indigenous ethnic groups and more indian reserves have been delimited; more limited land rights were outlined for black communities in the Pacific coastal region and cultural rights for blacks in general (Findji, 1992; Gros, 1991; Jackson, 1995).

As in the Nicaraguan case, real progress has been made, but again, there are limitations – more severe in a country where violence rules. In one sense, again, the concessions were forced from the state. Gros writes of the state's 'desire to instrumentalise an ethnic identity with the aim of negotiating its articulation with the dominant society' and a 'desire for modernisation and integration' (1994: 61, my translation). More to the point, for all the concessions they have on paper, indians now march for the 'right to life', as well as the right to land, because their leaders are being murdered by paramilitary death squads. Meanwhile, in the Pacific coastal region, 'development' proceeds regardless, with plans for roads and ports as well as colonisation on a more individual basis (Barnes, 1993).

However, an interesting aspect of the Colombian case, which is evident elsewhere, is the participation of indian and black leaders in formal electoral politics. Constitutional reform resulted, in December 1992, in three indian delegates being elected to Senate by a special indigenous constituency. Other indian leaders have also formed political parties, such as ASI (Alianza Social Indígena). Black communities were only allowed to elect delegates to the House of Representatives. In Ecuador in 1996, Luís Macas, the president of CONAIE (Confederación de Nacionalidades Indígenas del Ecuador) gained a seat as a Deputy in the National Congress, running on a Pachakutik-Nuevo País ticket. He sees this as an historic break with traditional politics, representing a truly grassroots driven democratic change and bringing together workers, Afro-Ecuadorians, women, youth, human rights workers and grassroots Christian communities.[7]

The impact of this participation is not entirely clear as yet, but so far it seems from Colombia's experience that the enthusiasm of Macas may not be fully justified. The process of co-optation into the machine of 'politics as normal' is a powerful danger as indigenous senators and representatives get sucked into the power play of dispensing patronage in exchange for votes. There is also the related threat of fragmentation as factions divide over control of votes and resources and over alliances with mainstream political parties. Indigenous leaders in Colombia talked of 'ethnicity getting out of control', as various indigenous groups manoeuvred for power.[8] Most importantly, although these political leaders act as a powerful antidote to standard images of blacks and indians, they are rather isolated in government and have little effective power. Nevertheless, the possible emergence of blacks and indians as real electoral forces, not easily channelled into traditional party politics, may have more radical longer-term effects if they are widely seen by the electorate as representing a real alternative for change.

In short, then, the adoption of official multiculturality needs to be examined long and hard, for it may easily be a tactical manoeuvre for coping with protest. In Asad's words: 'To secure its unity – to make its own history – dominant power has worked best through differentiating and classifying practices' (1993: 17).

Conclusion

This and the previous chapters have covered a wide variety of
issues and this is indicative of the direction in which the study
of racial and ethnic identities is going. No longer is it just a
question of race and class, or ethnicity and internal colonialism
– although these basic issues have not gone away by any
means. Now racial and ethnic identities must be seen in a
national and global context, as shifting, decentred, relational
constructions, subject to a politics of identity, culture and difference that encompasses gender, sexuality, religion and other
cultural expressions. In this unstable world, I wish to sound
two notes of warning. The first is to do with resistance, the
second with relationality and cultural continuity.

Imagining resistance

With the emergence of black and indian social movements, resistance has become a buzzword in anthropology and cultural studies. Interest in resistance goes back a long way, especially with
Marxist perspectives on exploitation, but today, in keeping with
the importance of investigating cultural politics, it has a broader
meaning. It is no longer simply a question of organised political
protest or even spontaneous but explicit protest. Foucault emphasised the connection of knowing to power and the ability of
power to construct people as subjects, rather than just govern
them. Power was, in his view, pervasive, rather than just concen-
trated in the hands of governors. Therefore, resistance could be
found wherever power operated. The influence of this approach,
combined with the impact of postcolonial 'subaltern studies', has
encouraged scholars to discover resistance – 'everyday resistance'
– in many activities not previously associated with this (see Abu-
Lughod, 1990, for a discussion). Any behaviour that seems not to
fit in with dominant definitions of what is right and proper can
be termed resistance and given political significance. The problem
with this is that resistance becomes virtually independent of the
intentions not only of the resistors, who may not think of things
in this way, but also of the perceptions of the oppressors: if no
one except the analyst can detect the resistance, then it is hard
to see what real political or even academic significance it has.

This is tricky ground, because to demand conscious awareness of resistance is to ignore the subtleties of the exercise of power that Foucault was precisely trying to uncover. Perhaps we can take our lead from Foucault himself who used to give parts of his work on the history of Western notions of discipline and punishment to French prisoners with the idea of promoting their own resistance. My point is that the acid test of relevance may be the reaction of the people studied to the information constructed by the observer about their resistance. If there is no recognition, either spontaneous or emergent, then perhaps the resistance is only in the imagination of the academic. This raises the difficult question of the political relation between the observer and the observed, and this I will tackle in the next chapter.

Relational identities

I have shown how over several decades the concept of identity has become more fluid and flexible. There are those, however, who question whether a completely relational approach over-emphasises this fluidity at the expense of real historical conti-nuities. This is not a question of denying relationality and returning to a pre-Barthian primordialist approach to ethnicity; it is simply a challenge to the idea that ethnicity is simply a boundary constituted by opposition and that the cultural stuff it contains is irrelevant. The problem, as Wilson puts it, is 'how to trace the history of the cultural dimension of ethnicity with-out relapsing into essentialism' (1995a: 10). The answer in his view – and my own – is supplied by Comaroff and Comaroff: the aim is to show how essences are constructed, 'how realities become real, how essences become essential' (1992: 20, cited by Wilson, 1995a: 10). For example, in the previous chapter's section about the power of blacks and indians, it is clear that the cultural stuff about the sexuality of blacks constitutes what Gilroy – who is concerned with the same problem – calls a 'changing same' (1993: 101), that is, a cultural complex that varies over time, but that shows real historical continuities that are relevant in the construction of relational identities (see also Wade, 1995b; Eriksen, 1991).

Of course, one of the features of new social movements is that they often take their own identity and their own culture very seriously. In fact, they frequently have a rather essentialist view of their own culture which, according to them, traces its roots continuously back through history and has an inner core which defines their identity. Now, while those with doubts about a radically relational approach to ethnic identity might be sympathetic to historical continuities, this is a subject for research, rather than just imagination. Thus, as an observer one can find oneself at odds with the people whose history and identity one is representing: they are not necessarily interested in showing how their essence became essential, but in rallying around that essence. If an anthropologist or historian shows that this essence is actually a rather variable thing, or does not have the characteristics it is supposed to have, in short deconstructs it, then s/he may find him or herself at odds with the people to whom such an essentialism is the basis of their identity. This, again, raises the question of the political relation between observer and observed and it is to this that I now turn.

7. STUDYING RACE AND ETHNICITY IN A POSTMODERN AND REFLEXIVE WORLD

Getting the Balance

Postmodernist approaches have made a great impact and have involved important challenges to the claims one can make to authoritative certainty, especially on behalf of others (including blacks and indians in Latin America). They have also emphasised the tendencies which already existed to see racial and ethnic identities as relational and shifting, rather than as reified objects. But with the insistence on relationality and the abandonment of metanarratives has come a strong measure of relativism and, at times, too great an emphasis on the process by which one person (usually the academic) represents another. This has led away from the invigorating attention to broad political and economic inequalities that was emblematic of the 1970s towards a more fragmented analysis that, while full of attention to power, tends to focus on the politics of poetics (for example, the politics of how texts are constructed and people represented in them), on the constant shiftings of cultural constructions and identities and on the micro-politics of the resistance that is detected – at times somewhat arbitrarily – in everyday behaviour. The politics of identity cannot be ignored – partly because it is important to blacks and indians in Latin America – but too exclusive a concentration on it seems to lead to an over-privileging of matters of discourse and representation, with issues of political economy (that is, how the product of society is created and distributed within it) being overwhelmed, despite their overriding importance for the many people who occupy a subordinate position in global and national society.

It should be obvious from my presentation in the preceding

chapter that a recognition of the flexibility of racial and ethnic identities, and of the importance of various dimensions of difference, does not necessarily lead away from central concerns with land, environment and power over resources: these remained important to most of the studies I cited. On the contrary, the trick is to retain both emphases and this has been a central theme of this book. This is not a question of combining 'culture' and 'economics'. These are not two separate realms that need to be balanced or combined; they are inseparable in that economics and politics and social life in general are lived *through* the medium of culture. Rather it is a question of seeing economics, politics, race and ethnicity as mutually influencing each other, rather than privileging one or two of these as determinative.

The early functionalist studies took social life seriously as an integrated whole – religion was as important as economics in constituting the 'identity' of the people concerned (although that word was not used) – but they assumed that each society was a neat whole and failed to question how communities (and identities) were constituted relationally; such relations were only really dealt with in terms of an imagined progression towards modernity. The UNESCO studies of race in Brazil and the later dependency and Marxist-oriented studies of the 1970s gave a good and necessary grip on the economics and politics of inequality – and, because capitalism was such a central focus, they did so in a way that vitally opened up the global and historical dimensions of inequality. But these studies subordinated race and ethnicity to class, as if race were superstructural 'culture', while class was infrastructural 'economics'. The mistake of subordinating race and ethnicity to class was a result of the mistake of equating race/ethnicity with culture and class with economics, as if race, ethnicity and class were not all lived through culture. Marxism typically failed to see that capitalist economics are constituted through culture not overlain by it.

Postmodernist approaches have helped here in that, for example, power is understood as constituted through discourse, rather than discourse simply being a representation of power, but this central insight has sometimes become submerged in, ironically, an over-emphasis on representation since, in practice, this becomes the images and texts through which discourse is most easily studied by academics. At the same time, the idea that discourses (and hence cultures) can be invented and that all culture is subject to constant re-invention is a useful insight into the flexibility of culture, but comes dangerously close to denying real historical continuities (Sahlins, 1993). The point is then to keep in view the basic concerns that racial and ethnic identities are involved with – resources, power, livelihood, autonomy and interdependence, knowledge of oneself and others, a sense of the past and the future – to see how these concerns are culturally constituted in an historical process and in relation to differences of power.

To give an example from my own work on blacks in Colombia: the small-scale study (after the functionalist style) of black communities is necessary to understand how they operate internally and to grasp the cultural modes through which their inhabitants live their lives. But it is not enough on its own. It is also fundamental to study (after the political economist's style) how black slaves underwrote the colonial economy, how blacks today act as labour in the cities and in rural areas and how the regions they inhabit act as 'internal colonies'; this permits us to grasp how they are located in the long-term distribution of power and resources (that is, dimensions of racial inequality). But this only tells half the story, seeing blackness as lain over or derivative of this underlying history. A more postmodernist approach might show how blackness has been constructed discursively, in different, changing ways by different sets of people (for example, whites, blacks, women, men), and how discourse involves power relations. But the danger lies in submerging oneself in discourse alone and the politics of competing representations. Black culture becomes subject to constant re-invention and negotiation and one loses sight of historical continuities. The aim, then, is to see – and this can only be done through ethnographic fieldwork – that the discursive construct of blackness is constantly recreated in social practices of colonisation and urban migration, of development plans and political processes such as constitutional reform, of sex and marriage, of music and sport; to see that blackness, whiteness and mixedness (and indianness) are values in their own right that form goals and enter into people's social interactions; they are connected to, but not simply derivative of, issues of economics and politics; to see that historical continuity is constituted through constant change, as the same kinds of relations and expressions are remade with ever-changing cultural resources (Sahlins, 1993).

In sum, it is not a question of returning to pre-postmodernist perspectives, but of encompassing the useful insights of postmodernist perspectives while avoiding a headlong rush into the arms of total relativism, into the endlessly shifting sands of a radical cultural constructionism that undoes historical continuity, or into the realms where discourse ceases to be a social practice that engages people in a real world.

Being Reflexive

The foregoing discussion deals with a problem of balance. A different problem of balance, which has been raised forcefully by postmodernist critiques, is that between the person carrying out a study and those s/he is studying and I think it is necessary to address this head on.

One of the features of a postmodern world has been the increasing reflexivity of social life. This is the way that society 'feeds back' on itself so that changes produced in one place spread quickly in a global fashion. Specifically, it includes the way knowledge produced by specialists feeds back into the contexts from which they derived that knowledge. Thus, for example, sociological theories about marriage or political behaviour inform, usually via the media, people's decisions about how to behave in those domains. This means that social 'scientists' can hardly hope to arrive at law-like generalisations about human behaviour, since their generalisations change the thing they were generalising about (Giddens, 1990). It also means that their studying and theorising can have important political effects. In the study of blacks and indians, it involves the fact that the people being studied are increasingly able to access, evaluate and be influenced (or not) by the work produced about them. Radio and television are pervasive and, for example, Kayapo indians in Brazilian Amazonia both view and make films about themselves (Turner, 1992). More than a few black and indian leaders in Latin America have studied anthropology and ethnolinguistics and, for example, 'Guatemalan Maya intellectuals and professionals ... have begun demanding the return of their heritage, their history and their identity – from anthropologists [and] ... from their own country' (Watanabe, 1995).

In a world that is not only postmodern but postcolonial, the authority of the work produced by, say, anthropologists about others ('natives') is doubly questioned: not only do the 'natives' have increasing access to the work, but the status of knowledge in general is less certain and its ties to the social location of the people producing it more evident. Therefore, the relationship of academics to the people they study becomes a lot more complex than realised in previous decades.

In the 1980s, anthropologists worried over this by analysing their ethnographic practice – fieldwork and writing up. Indeed, 'reflexivity' came to mean anthropologists reflecting on ethnographic texts, leading to an excess of navel-gazing that distracted attention from the more general meaning of reflexivity, that is, the reflexive social relation between the anthropologist and the anthropologised. In this anxious self-examination, ethnographic writing could be seen, like the work of fiction, to be laden with particular rhetorical 'devices', in this case, ones of distancing and authorisation which subtly gave the anthropologist narrative authority. Part of the answer to this was, then, to write in different ways, particularly to write 'multivocal' ethnographies in which the people being studied 'spoke for themselves'. This has some real advantages in conveying a sense of the people studied as active agents (see for example Whitten, 1985), but of course it was still the anthropologist who decided what was included and excluded from the final text (Clifford and Marcus, 1986; Marcus and Fischer, 1986; Watanabe, 1995). This inequality of control is ultimately predicated on the uneven global distribution of control over the means of production of knowledge (research funding, universities, publishing) and therefore cannot be easily cast aside.

So the problem remains of the political relationship between observer and observed. One approach to this is to engage in advocacy – a well-established anthropological tactic. This is narrowly defined as speaking on behalf of others, who by definition are less able to do so for themselves in particular contexts (such as legal proceedings, or in official circles). More broadly, it involves promoting the cause of particular groups through publicity and campaigning. More generally still, it can include the promotion of certain basic principles – of anti-racism, respect for cultural difference – through writing, teaching, film-making and so on.

Advocacy is full of problems. Some think it is at odds with anthropology (or social science) as an enterprise, since the latter seeks to grasp an overall context, while advocacy seeks to promote one particular set of interests. There are also endless problems of *whose* interests one represents – an 'indigenous community' is rarely unified in this respect (Hastrup and Elsass, 1990; Paine, 1985). However, I do not think these problems mean that advocacy should be abandoned. Any political engagement is bound to be conflictive and unclear; one has to make decisions, about what to advocate on whose behalf, which are basically value judgements, even if these are informed by anthropological knowledge. In practice, of course, advocacy in its

various forms is widespread, whether through groups such as
Survival International (which was inspired by the plight of
Amazonian indians) or the International Working Group for
Indigenous Affairs (IWGIA), through the participation of anthro-
pologists as advisers/campaigners in constitutional reform in
Colombia or Nicaragua (Arocha, 1992; Scherrer, 1994: 115), or
through video projects among the Kayapo (Turner, 1992).

Another set of problems arises when representations produced
by an anthropologist or a historian about a particular group and its
culture come into conflict with representations produced by that
group, or more likely a literate elite of the group. A clear example
of this comes from outside the Latin American context. One US
scholar of the New Zealand Maori showed that the cultural history
of the Maori purveyed by Maori intellectuals depended on certain
versions of that history produced by Western scholars in the nineteenth century which were actually 'wrong'; thus Maori identity
depended partly on an 'invented tradition', a term made famous by
Hobsbawm and Ranger (1983). The press snapped up his academic
article, ran headlines saying 'US scholar says Maori culture is
invented' and Maori cultural activists got very annoyed (Hanson,
1989, 1991). For Mayan ethnic revivalist movements, Watanabe
notes that 'In direct contrast to many recent "constructionist"
studies of Maya ethnicity, ... many pan-Mayanists explore the possibilities of an "essentialist" Maya identity' (1995: 37).

These examples raise questions of authenticity. 'Authentic'
means simply 'true', but it also means original, good and whole-
some. The traditions at stake in cases like these are not just
factually accurate or inaccurate, they underwrite people's identities – and perhaps land claims. Identities are often represented
by cultural activists in an essentialist way that may be based on
history: 'Essentialism is the affirmation of common style, quality,
and culture – the oneness of a people – that revitalises a sense of
historical depth' (Whitten, 1985: 230). The indigenist revivalism
evident in Guatemala is a good example of essentialist representations with its 'radical view of ethnicity' that 'encourages the
renovation of aspects of traditional religion and culture, and ...
asserts the superiority of indigenous peoples over nonindigenous'
(Wilson, 1995a: 260). When academics deconstruct these historical traditions or more generally when they show how 'essential-
isms become essential', they may be weakening those identities
and claims. As black sociologist Paul Gilroy says, 'some of us ...
are just beginning to formulate our own big narratives precisely
as narratives of redemption and emancipation', and the decon-

struction of history and metanarratives would seem to be at odds with this (cited in Keith and Cross, 1993: 23).

So how should anthropologists and historians react in these cases? I think it is necessary to maintain some notion of 'truth' – or rather falsity. We do want to be able to say that certain ideas about Maori culture are factually incorrect, according to the normal canons of historical investigation. Equally, I do want to be able to contest the representation of Latin American blacks as indomitable resisters that is invoked in ideologies of *cimarronismo*, which hold up the image of the runaway slave and the runaway slave community as the true essence of Colombian, or Brazilian, black history and black identity. There is another side to black history in which freed blacks owned black slaves and *cimarrones* worked on nearby haciendas and asked for Catholic priests to visit (Wade, 1993a: 87–8).

The answer to the dilemma, or part of an answer, is precisely to engage in the reflexivity that uncovered the whole problem in the first place. Essentialist representations are political statements, as are the deconstructions of them; so it is possible to have a dialogue between them. It is probably unhelpful to talk the language of 'invention', because all human culture is invented in some sense and there is no effective distinction between 'genuine' and 'spurious' culture (Jackson, 1995). But it is possible to juxtapose and discuss different versions of events and identities and to take those versions as political agendas with political effects that can be debated. Thus to represent indians as the 'natural' guardians of the earth – an image which can be deployed by indians and non-indians alike – may have the effect of locking them into conservation, while many of them may want development.[1]

A dialogue along these lines is not easy. Black activists in Colombia read some of the material I produce about blacks in that country (since some of it I write in Spanish) and sometimes we have discussions about it. The question of Africanisms often comes up, because one current of black activism and indeed of anthropology in Colombia seeks to discover the African roots of black culture, not just as an historical investigation, but as a political endeavour. I take a less Herskovitsian line, by no means denying Africanisms, but pointing out that undue emphasis on them can act to exclude the large parts of black culture which are evidently not African-derived. For Guatemala, Watanabe notes that 'Maya ... ask ethnographers how to better anthropologise themselves for their own ends'; they want advice on how to study themselves to achieve 'some kind of Maya anthropology by Maya for Maya' which is not, however, independent of non-Maya anthropologists (1995: 40, 39). Turner (1991) notes that the interest of anthropologists in Kayapo culture helped draw the attention of the Kapayo themselves to their own culture and the possibility of representing and objectifying it. So there is some debate and dialogue.

There is no point being romantic about this and pretending the power relations that have traditionally differentiated the studiers from the studied are about to be overturned. My anthropological dialogue with blacks in Colombia is very limited: by the small number of black intellectuals and their restricted access to libraries, by my own location in a (distant) academic environment that does not give much value to such dialogue, and so on. It is fashionable nowadays to pay homage to reflexivity, but the real inequalities of power that exist still militate against it.

Nevertheless, the future for the study of race and ethnicity in Latin America will perforce be one of increasing reflexivity, of blacks and indians producing their own versions of their history and identity and engaging in debates with academics, as well as government officials, about these. This, I think, is not wishful thinking, but a simple fact. The process would be facilitated by a more equal distribution of the means of production of knowledge – and here Latin America has a head-start on, say, Africa, in that it has well-established academy. This is not to say, by any means, that the means of production of knowledge are equally distributed within Latin American nations, but there is a greater chance for dialogue between Latin American academics and black and indian social movements, just as there is some chance for blacks and indians – albeit not many – to enter the academy if they want to and can get to its gates.[2]

In an environment in which those who traditionally have been the 'objects' of enquiry begin to study themselves in academic mode, the boundaries between different kinds of knowledge may become less clear and indeed what counts as (social scientific) knowledge at all may be questioned.

Whitten recounts an encounter between Sicuanga, a Quichua indian, and a local schoolteacher, in discussions about local land conflicts. At one point, the former began tell mythical stories, 'seemingly out of context', about the doings of ancestors. The teacher 'had glimmers of what Sicuanga's message meant, and he knew that there was something profound there if he could only grasp it' (1985: 251). Part of that message was that there might be other ways of approaching the future than 'development' and 'modernisation', of owning the land as property and subjecting it to ever-increasing productivity. In that sense, these other kinds of knowledge constitute a critique of Western modernity (Zanotta Machado, 1994), even if the critique is not always phrased in the language of modernity. Part of anthropology's task has always been the translation between cultures, opening Sicuanga's mythicalhicalicalcalall discourse to outsiders by translating it into social scientific and/or popular terminology. This task will take on more complex dimensions if some anthropologists themselves start to use mythical discourse, claiming it as a legitimate equal to analytic language. Here is where the relativism of postmodernity will not serve us well: anthropology may point up cultural difference but it has lost its purpose if it ceases also to mediate and translate across that difference.

NOTES

Introduction

1. I would like to thank Jenny Pearce and Françoise Barbira-Freedman for their helpful comments during the process of writing this book.

1. The Meaning of 'Race' and 'Ethnicity'

1. There is, of course, a parallel here with the 'observer effect' in natural sciences, in which the process of observation disturbs the thing being observed. In the social sciences, however, this takes on a different, less predictable dimension. For a discussion of all these themes, see Kuhn's classic text (Kuhn, 1970); see also Giddens (1976).
2. There are many sources on the history of the concept of race. See, for example, Banton (1987), Barkan (1992), Reynolds and Lieberman (1996), Smedley (1993), Stepan (1982).
3. In fact, Jordan (1977: 18–19) says that the Bible itself gave no grounds for linking Africans with the sons of Ham; these grounds came from Talmudic and Midrashic scriptural sources.
4. Between 1802 and 1820, slave trading was abolished by Denmark, Britain, the US, Sweden, Holland and France. Illegal slave trading by some of these countries nevertheless continued thereafter. Although there were prohibitions on slave trading enacted by or forced on Spain and Portugal during this period, Brazil, Puerto Rico and Cuba continued to import slaves until about the 1870s. Slavery itself was abolished in the Spanish ex-colonies between 1824 and 1854 (except in Puerto Rico and Cuba where it persisted until 1873 and 1886, respectively), although many countries had previously enacted 'free womb laws' that freed children subsequently born to slave mothers. Slavery ceased in Brazil in 1888, while between 1838 and 1863 it ended in Britain, France, Denmark, the US and finally Holland. See Curtin (1969).
5. I will not always put the term 'black' in inverted commas in this book, but it should be borne in mind that it is nothing more than a shorthand term of reference for a variable category.

Notes

6. Frankenberg (1993) finds that many white Americans do not consider themselves to have a 'racial identity' – for them, this is something only 'others' have. But Nell Berstein reports that Anglo-American teenagers in California actively claim a minority racial identity (Hispanic, black), based on dress and music styles ('Goin' gansta, choosin' cholita', reproduced in *The UTNE Reader*, March–April 1995, pp. 87–90).
7. This may seem to ignore that ideas about 'race' also exist in Japan – closely connected to its own imperial history – and also in China. In both cases, however, the impact of European writings from the nineteenth century onwards was influential in affecting the way Japanese and Chinese thinkers conceived of human difference (Weiner, 1995; Dikötter, 1991). This is not to say, however, that thinking in terms of 'blood' and other bodily essences as defining differences is uniquely European. The point is that it is primarily in Europe (and the US) that the whole ideology of race was most elaborated.
8. Reported in 'Goin' gansta, choosin' cholita', by Nell Bernstein; reproduced in *The UTNE Reader*, March–April 1995, pp. 87–90.
9. This raises the problem of how national identities relate to ethnic ones (see Eriksen 1993). Briefly, a nation is an ethnic group that seeks political sovereignty over the territory of which it claims cultural ownership and control; a nation-state exists when that sovereignty is achieved. Of course, such a claim to ownership and control on the part of one group may be contested by other groups who see themselves as different but occupy, or wish to control, parts of the same territory.

2. Blacks and Indians in Latin America

1. In this book, I use the term 'indian' to refer to the indigenous peoples of the Americas. Many people avoid this term, since the Spanish and Portuguese term *indio* is often used pejoratively in Latin America. Alternative terms include indigenous people, Amerindians and native Americans. I continue to use the term 'indian', partly because I think it does not have the same pejorative connotation in English, but also to put the terms 'black' and 'indian' on the same footing (hence the non-capitalisation of the word) where I believe they belong. Neither term indicates a national grouping, both are culturally constructed and vary over space and time.
2. Hendrickson (1991: 290) notes that in Guatemala the categories 'indian' and 'ladino' (mestizo) are referred to explicitly as labels of *raza* (race) as well as ethnic group. Many authors note that indians face 'racism', even while they refer to them as ethnic groups (for example, Harris, 1995b: 371; Whitten, 1976; Watanabe, 1995).

121

3. Early Approaches to Blacks and Indians, 1920s–1960s

1. These data are available on *Folha*'s web pages, located at http://www.embratel.net.br/infoserv/agfolha/datafolh/index.html.

4. Inequality and Situational Identity: 1970s

1. Whitten uses the 'Quechua' spelling in his 1975 text and 'Quichua' thereafter.
2. See also Brandon (1993), Gilroy (1993a), Palmié (1995), Price (1979), Whitten and Szwed (1970) for different discussions of the problems involved in ideas of African 'traditions'.

5. Blacks and Indians in the Postmodern Nation-State

1. Useful introductions to postmodernism and postmodernity include Giddens (1990), Hall, Held and McGrew (1992), Harvey (1989), Turner (1990). For Latin America, see Beverley, Oviedo and Aronna (1995).
2. Both Derrida and Foucault actually wrote many of their works in the 1960s. Much of this was not translated into English until the 1970s and 1980s, however, and their impact on social science has been mainly from the 1980s.
3. The use of spatial metaphors in some of the recent literature reflects a general concern in social theory with the spatial dimensions of social relations, but it has been especially attractive in Latin America where minorities are often engaged in a concrete struggle for land rights as part of their cultural space.
4. See Kizca (1995) for a review of recent ethnohistorical work on Mexico.
5. See also Smith (1990), Stavenhagen (1996).
6. This is the subject of a book in preparation by myself and Egberto Bermúdez.

6. Black and Indian Social Movements

1. For black resistance, see Guss (1996), Heuman (1986), Price (1979, 1983), Taussig (1980), Whitten and Torres (1992). For indian resistance, see Stern (1987), Rivera Cusicanqui (1993), Mallon (1992), Rappaport (1990, 1994), Gosner and Ouweneel (1996); Larson, Harris and Tandeter (1995) also have many references to the ethnohistorical work on Andean resistance. See also Field (1994), Kizca (1995), Hill (1996).

2. For Latin America generally, see Field (1994), Mallon (1992), and the special issue of *Latin American Perspectives* on Ethnicity and Class in Latin America, vol. 23, no. 2, Spring 1996. See also the special journal issue: 'Gaining ground: the indigenous movement in Latin America', *NACLA Report on the Americas*, 29(5), March/April 1996. For Colombia, see Findji (1992), Gros (1991), Jackson (1995). For Guatemala, see Watanabe (1995), Wilson (1995a). For Mexico, see Campbell (1995), Nash (1995). For Ecuador, see Whitten (1985: ch. 6), Zamosc (1994). For the Brazilian Amazon, see Branford and Glock (1985: ch. 5), Fisher (1994), Turner (1991).

3. The first quotation is from a communiqué issued by the EZLN on its twelfth anniversary in November 1995, circulated on the Internet by Acción Zapatista (http://www.utexas.edu/ftp/student/nave). The second is from a communiqué of January 1994, cited in Renard (1994: 13). See also Nash (1995).

4. See also Stepan (1991), Parker et al. (1992), and Yuval-Davis and Anthias (1989).

5. Reported in an interview from *Turning the Tide*, Sept/Oct 1994, circulated on the Internet by Acción Zapatista (http://www.utexas.edu/ftp/student/nave/ep6.html).

6. On Colombia, see Wade (1995a), Arocha (1992); 'Ethnicity reconfigured: indigenous legislators and the Colombian constitution of 1991', *Journal of Latin American Anthropology* 1(2), Spring 1996; on Bolivia and Brazil, Zanotta Machado (1994); on Nicaragua, Vilas (1989), Hale (1994); for various Latin American countries, see Assies and Hoekema (1994). See also the special journal issue: 'Gaining ground: the indigenous movement in Latin America', *NACLA Report on the Americas*, 29(5), March/April 1996.

7. See the interview with Luís Macas in the journal of the South and Meso-American Indian Rights Center, *Abya Yala News* 10(2), Summer 1996, published on-line at http://www.maxwell.syr.edu/nativeweb/ab-yayala/orgs/saiic/ayn/index.htmtl. vol. 8(3), Fall 1994, of this journal is a special issue on 'Indian Movements and the Electoral Process'. On CONAIE, see Zamosc (1994).

8. Leon Zamosc, personal communication, based on interviews with indigenous leaders in Colombia in 1993.

7. *Studying Race and Ethnicity in a Postmodern and Reflexive World*

1. See Ellen (1986) on myths of 'Green primitivism'.
2. In Colombia, for example, the National University has special funded places set aside for students from indigenous communities.

BIBLIOGRAPHY

Abercrombie, Thomas (1991) 'To be Indian, to be Bolivian: "ethnic" and "national" discourses of identity', in Greg Urban and Joel Sherzer (eds) *Nation-States and Indians in Latin America*, pp. 95–130 (Austin: University of Texas Press).

Abu–Lughod, Lila (1990) 'The romance of resistance: tracing transformations of power through Bedouin women', *American Ethnologist* 17(1): 41–55.

Aguirre Beltrán, Gonzalo (1979) *Regions of Refuge* (Washington: Society for Applied Anthropology).

Alden, Dauril (1987) 'Late colonial Brazil, 1750–1808', in Leslie Bethell (ed.), *Colonial Brazil*, pp. 283–343 (Cambridge: Cambridge University Press).

Amos, V. and P. Parmar (1984) 'Challenging imperial feminism', *Feminist Review* 17: 3–19.

Anderson, Benedict (1983) *Imagined Communities: Reflections on the Origin and Spread of Nationalism* (London: Verso).

Andrews, George Reid (1991) *Blacks and Whites in São Paulo, Brazil, 1888–1988* (Madison: University of Wisconsin Press).

Andrews, George Reid (1992) 'Black political protest in São Paulo, 1888–1988', *Journal of Latin American Studies* 24: 147–71.

Anthias, Floya and Nira Yuval-Davis (1992) *Racialized Boundaries: Race, Nation, Gender, Colour and Class and the Anti-Racist Struggle* (London: Routledge).

Arocha, Jaime (1992) 'Afro-Colombia denied', *NACLA Report on the Americas* 25(4): 28–31.

Asad, Talal (1993) *Genealogies of Religion: Discipline and Reasons of Power in Christianity and Islam* (Baltimore: Johns Hopkins University Press).

Assies, W.J. and A.J. Hoekema (eds) (1994) *Indigenous Peoples' Experiences with Self-Government* (Amsterdam: IWGIA and the University of Amsterdam).

Azevedo, Thales de (1953) *Les élites de couleur dans une ville brésilienne* (Paris: UNESCO).

Banks, Marcus (1996) *Ethnicity: Anthropological Constructions* (London: Routledge).

Banton, Michael (1967) *Race Relations* (London: Tavistock).

Banton, Michael (1983) *Racial and Ethnic Competition* (Cambridge: Cambridge University Press).

Banton, Michael (1987) *Racial Theories* (Cambridge: Cambridge University Press).

Barbira-Freedman, Françoise (ed.) (1980) *Land, People and Planning in Contemporary Amazonia* (Cambridge: Centre of Latin American Studies, University of Cambridge).

Barkan, Elazar (1992) *The Retreat of Scientific Racism: Changing Concepts of Race in Britain and the United States between the World Wars* (Cambridge: Cambridge University Press).

Barkan, Elazar (1996) 'The politics of the science of race: Ashley Montagu and UNESCO's anti-racist declarations', in L.T. Reynolds and L. Lieberman (eds) *Race and Other Misadventures: Essays in Honor of Ashley Montagu in his Ninetieth Year*, pp. 96–105 (Dix Hills, NY: General Hall Inc.).

Barker, Martin (1981) *The New Racism* (London: Junction Books).

Barnes, Jon (1993) 'Driving roads through land rights: the Colombian Plan Pacífico', *Ecologist* 23(4): 135–40.

Barth, Frederick (ed.) (1969) *Ethnic Groups and Boundaries: The Social Organisation of Cultural Difference* (London: George Allen and Unwin).

Bastide, Roger (1957) 'Race relations in Brazil', *International Social Science Bulletin* 9: 495–512.

Bastide, Roger (1961) 'Dusky Venus, black Apollo', *Race* 3: 10–19.

Bastide, Roger (1971) *African Civilizations in the New World* (London: C. Hurst).

Bastide, Roger (1978) *African Religions of Brazil: Towards a Sociology of the Interpenetration of Civilizations* (Baltimore: Johns Hopkins University Press).

Bastide, Roger and Florestan Fernandes (1955) *Relações raciais entre negroes e brancos em São Paulo* (São Paulo: Editora Anhembí).

Bauer, Arnold (1984) 'Rural Spanish America, 1870–1930', in Leslie Bethell (ed.) *The Cambridge History of Latin America*, vol. 4, pp. 151–86 (Cambridge: Cambridge University Press).

Béhague, Gerard (ed.) (1994) *Music and Black Ethnicity: The Caribbean and South America* (New Brunswick: Transaction Publishers).

Beverley, John, José Oviedo and Michael Aronna (eds) (1995) *The Postmodernism Debate in Latin America* (Durham: Duke University Press).

Blauert, Jutta and Marta Guidi (1992) 'Strategies for auto-chthonous development: two initiatives in rural Oaxaca, Mexico', in Dhoram Ghai and Jessica Vivian (eds) *Grassroots Environmental Action: People's Participation in Sustainable Development*, pp. 188–220 (London: Routledge).

Bourricaud, François (1975) 'Indian, mestizo and cholo as symbols in the Peruvian system of stratification', in Nathan Glazier and Daniel Moynihan (eds) *Ethnicity: Theory and Experience*, pp. 350–87 (Cambridge, Mass.: Harvard University Press).

Bowser, Frederick (1972) 'Colonial Spanish America', in David Cohen and Jack Greene (eds) *Neither Slave nor Free: Freedmen of African Descent in the Slave Societies of the New World*, pp. 19–58 (Baltimore: Johns Hopkins University Press).

Brading, David (1988) 'Manuel Gamio and official *indigenismo*', *Bulletin of Latin American Research* 7(1): 75–90.

Brandon, George (1993) *Santería from Africa to the New World: The Dead Sell Memories* (Bloomington: Indiana University Press).

Branford, Sue and Oriel Glock (1985) *The Last Frontier: Fighting over Land in the Amazon* (London: Zed Books).

Brown, Diana (1986) *Umbanda: Religion and Politics in Brazil* (Ann Arbor: UMI Research Press).

Brysk, Alison (1996) 'Turning weakness into strength: the inter-nationalization of Indian rights', *Latin American Perspectives*, special issue on Ethnicity and Class in Latin America, 23(2): 38–57.

Bueno, Salvador (1993) 'The black and white in the narrative of Alejo Carpentier', in Pedro Pérez Sarduy and Jean Stubbs (eds) *Afro-Cuba: An Anthology of Cuban Writing on Race, Politics and Culture*, pp. 214–21 (London: Latin American Bureau).

Burdick, John (1992a) 'Brazil's black consciousness movement', *NACLA Report on the Americas* 25(4): 23–7.

Burdick, John (1992b) 'Rethinking the study of social movements: the case of Christian Base Communities in urban Brazil', in Arturo Escobar and Sonia Alvarez (eds) *The Making of Social Movements in Latin America: Identity, Strategy and Democracy*, pp. 171–84 (Boulder: Westview Press).

Campbell, Howard (1995) *Zapotec Renaissance: Ethnic Politics and Cultural Revivalism in Southern Mexico* (Albuquerque: University of New Mexico Press).

Carby, Hazel (1982) 'White women listen! Black feminists and the boundaries of sisterhood', in The Centre for Contemporary Cultural Studies (ed.) *The Empire Strikes Back: Race and Racism in 70s Britain*, pp. 212–36 (London: Hutchinson and CCCS, Birmingham University).

Cardoso, Fernando Henrique and Octavio Ianni (1960) *Côr e mobilidade social em Florianópolis* (São Paulo: Companhia Editora Nacional).

Carroll, Patrick (1991) *Blacks in Colonial Veracruz: Race, Ethnicity and Regional Development* (Austin: University of Texas Press).

Castellanos, Jorge and Isabel Castellanos (1990) *Cultura afrocubana*. vol. 2. *El negro en Cuba, 1845–1959* (Miami: Ediciones Universal).

Chance, John (1978) *Race and Class in Colonial Oaxaca* (Stanford: Stanford University Press).

Chevalier, François (1970) 'Official *indigenismo* in Peru in 1920: origins, significance and socioeconomic scope', in Magnus Mörner (ed.) *Race and Class in Latin America*, pp. 184–96 (New York: Columbia University Press).

Clifford, James and George Marcus (eds) (1986) *Writing Culture: The Poetics and Politics of Ethnography* (Berkeley: University of California Press).

Cohen, Abner (1969) *Custom and Politics in Urban Africa: A Study of Hausa Migrants in Yoruba Towns* (London: Routledge and Kegan Paul).

Cohen, Abner (ed.) (1974) *Urban Ethnicity* (London: Tavistock).

Colby, Benjamin and Pierre van den Berghe (1961) 'Ethnic relations in southeastern Mexico', *American Anthropologist* 63: 772–92.

Colby, Benjamin and Pierre van den Berghe (1969) *Ixil Country: A Plural Society in Highland Guatemala* (Berkeley: University of California Press).

Collinson, Helen (ed.) (1996) *Green Guerrillas: Environmental Conflicts and Initiatives in Latin America and the Caribbean* (London: Latin American Bureau).

Comaroff, John and Jean Comaroff (1992) *Ethnography and the Historical Imagination* (Boulder: Westview Press).

Curtin, Philip (1969) *The Atlantic Slave Trade: A Census* (Madison: University of Wisconsin Press).

Davis, David Brion (1969) 'A comparison of British America and Latin America', in Laura Foner and Eugene Genovese (eds) *Slavery in the New World: A Reader in Comparative History*, pp. 69–83 (Englewood Cliffs, NJ: Prentice-Hall).

Davis, Shelton (1977) *Victims of the Miracle: Development and the Indians of Brazil* (Cambridge: Cambridge University Press).

de la Cadena, Marisol (1995) '"Women are more Indian": ethnicity and gender in a community near Cuzco', in Brooke Larson, Olivia Harris and Enrique Tandeter (eds) *Ethnicity, Markets and Migration in the Andes: At the Crossroads of History and Anthropology*, pp. 329–48 (Durham: Duke University Press).

de la Fuente, Julio (1965) *Relaciones interétnicas* (Mexico: Instituto Nacional Indigenista).

Degler, Carl (1971) *Neither Black nor White: Slavery and Race Relations in Brazil and the United States* (New York: Macmillan).

Díaz Ayala, Cristóbal (1981) *La música cubana: del Areyto a la nueva trova* (San Juan, Puerto Rico: Ediciones Cubanacan).

Dikötter, Frank (1991) *The Discourse of Race in Modern China* (London: Hurst).

Doughty, Paul (1972) 'Peruvian migrant identity in the urban milieu', in Thomas Weaver and Douglas White (eds) *The Anthropology of Urban Environments*, pp. 39–50 (Washington: Society for Applied Anthropology).

Drucker-Brown, Susan (ed.) (1982) *Malinowski in Mexico: The Economics of a Mexican Market System*, by Bronislaw Malinowski and Julio de la Fuente (London: Routledge and Kegan Paul. Original edition: Mexico, 1957).

Dzidzienyo, Anani (1979) 'The position of blacks in Brazilian society', in A. Dzidzienyo and Lourdes Casal, *The Position of Blacks in Brazilian and Cuban Society*, pp. 2–11 (London: Minority Rights Group).

Ellen, Roy (1986) 'What Black Elk left unsaid: on the illusory images of Green primitivism', *Anthropology Today* 2(6): 8–13.

Elsass, Peter (1992) *Strategies for Survival: The Psychology of Cultural Resilience in Ethnic Minorities* (New York: New York University Press).

Eltis, David (1987) *Economic Growth and the Ending of the Transatlantic Slave Trade* (Oxford: Oxford University Press).

Epstein, A.L. (1978) *Ethos and Identity* (London: Tavistock).

Eriksen, Thomas Hylland (1991) 'The cultural contexts of ethnic differences', *Man* 26(1): 127–44.

Eriksen, Thomas Hylland (1993) *Ethnicity and Nationalism: Anthropological Perspectives* (London: Pluto Press).

Escobar, Arturo (1992a) 'Culture, economics, and politics in Latin American social movements theory and research', in Arturo Escobar and Sonia Alvarez (eds) *The Making of Social*

Movements in Latin America: Identity, Strategy and Democracy, pp. 62–85 (Boulder: Westview Press).

Escobar, Arturo (1992b) 'Culture, practice and politics: anthropology and the study of social movements', *Critique of Anthropology* 12(4): 395–432.

Escobar, Arturo and Sonia E. Alvarez (eds) (1992) *The Making of Social Movements in Latin America: Identity, Strategy, and Democracy* (Boulder: Westview Press).

Fernandes, Florestan (1969) *The Negro in Brazilian Society*, translated from the Portuguese by J.D. Skiles, A. Brunel and A. Rothwell and edited by Phyllis Eveleth (New York: Colombia University Press).

Fernandes, Florestan (1979) 'The Negro in Brazil: twenty-five years later', in M. Margolies and W. Carter (eds) *Brazil: Anthropological Perspectives*, pp. 96–114 (New York: Columbia University Press).

Field, Les W. (1994) 'Who are the Indians?: reconceptualizing indigenous identity, resistance and the role of social science in Latin America', *Latin American Research Review* 29(3): 237–48.

Findji, María Teresa (1992) 'From resistance to social movement: the Indigenous Authorities Movement in Colombia', in Arturo Escobar and Sonia Alvarez (eds) *The Making of Social Movements in Latin America: Identity, Strategy and Democracy*, pp. 112–33 (Boulder: Westview Press).

Fisher, William H. (1994) 'Megadevelopment, environmentalism, and resistance: the institutional context of Kayapó indigenous politics in central Brazil', *Human Organization* 53(3): 220–32.

Foner, Laura and Eugene Genovese (eds) (1969) *Slavery in the New World: A Reader in Comparative History* (Englewood Cliffs, NJ: Prentice-Hall Inc.).

Fontaine, Pierre-Michel (1980) 'The political economy of Afro-Latin America', *Latin American Research Review* 15(2): 111–41.

Fontaine, Pierre-Michel (1981) 'Transnational relations and racial mobilisation: emerging black movements in Brazil', in John F. Stack (ed.) *Ethnic Identities in a Transnational World*, pp. 141–62 (Westport: Greenwood Press).

Foster, George (1967) *Tzintzuntzan: Mexican Peasants in a Changing World* (Boston: Little, Brown and Company).

Foweraker, Joe (1995) *Theorising Social Movements* (London: Pluto Press).

Franco, Jean (1967) *The Modern Culture of Latin America: Society and the Artist* (London: Pall Mall Press).

Race and Ethnicity in Latin America

Frankenberg, Ruth (1993) *White Women, Race Matters: The Social Construction of Whiteness* (London: Routledge).

Freeland, Jane (1995) 'Nicaragua', in Minority Rights Group (ed.) *No Longer Invisible: Afro-Latin Americans Today*, pp. 181–201 (London: Minority Rights Group).

Freyre, Gilberto (1951) *Brazil: An Interpretation* (New York: Alfred Knopf).

Freyre, Gilberto (1959) *New World in the Tropics: The Culture of Modern Brazil* (New York: Alfred Knopf).

Friedemann, Nina de (1984) 'Estudios de negros en la antropología colombiana', in Jaime Arocha and Nina Friedemann (eds) *Un siglo de investigación en Colombia*, pp. 507–72 (Bogotá: Etno).

Friedemann, Nina de and Jaime Arocha (1986) *De sol a sol: génesis, transformación y presencia de los negros en Colombia* (Bogotá: Planeta).

Friedemann, Nina de and Jaime Arocha (1995) 'Colombia', in Minority Rights Group (ed.), *No Longer Invisible: Afro-Latin Americans Today*, pp. 47–76 (London: Minority Rights Group).

Friedlander, Judith (1975) *Being Indian in Hueyapan: A Study of Forced Identity in Contemporary Mexico* (New York: St Martins Press).

García Canclini, Néstor (1989) *Culturas híbridas: estrategias para entrar y salir de la modernidad* (Mexico: Grijalbo).

Giddens, Anthony (1976) *New Rules of Sociological Method: A Positive Critique of Interpretative Sociologies* (London: Hutchinson).

Giddens, Anthony (1987) *Social Theory and Modern Society* (Cambridge: Polity Press).

Giddens, Anthony (1990) *The Consequences of Modernity* (Cambridge: Polity Press).

Gillin, John (1951) *The Culture of Security in San Carlos: A Study of a Guatemalan Community of Indians and Ladinos* (New Orleans: Middle American Research Institute, Tulane University).

Gilroy, Paul (1982) 'Steppin' out of Babylon: race, class and autonomy', in The Centre for Contemporary Cultural Studies (ed.) *The Empire Strikes Back: Race and Racism in 70s Britain*, pp. 276–314 (London: Hutchinson and CCCS, Birmingham University).

Gilroy, Paul (1987) *'There Ain't no Black in the Union Jack': The Cultural Politics of Race and Nation* (London: Hutchinson).

Gilroy, Paul (1993a) *The Black Atlantic: Modernity and Double Consciousness* (London: Verso).

Gilroy, Paul (1993b) *Small Acts: Thoughts on the Politics of Black Cultures* (London: Serpent's Tail).

Glazer, Nathan and Daniel Moynihan (eds) (1975) *Ethnicity: Theory and Experience* (Cambridge: Harvard University Press).

Goldberg, D. (1993) *Racist Culture: Philosophy and the Politics of Meaning* (Oxford: Blackwell).

González, Lélia (1985) 'The Unified Black Movement: a new stage in black political mobilization', in Pierre-Michel Fontaine (ed.) *Race, Class and Power in Brazil*, pp. 120–34 (Los Angeles: Center for Afro-American Studies, University of California).

González Casanova, Pablo (1971) *La sociología de la explotación* (Mexico: Siglo XXI).

Gose, Peter (1984) *Deathly Waters and Hungry Mountains: Agrarian Ritual and Class Formation in an Andean Town* (Toronto: University of Toronto Press).

Gosner, Kevin and Arij Ouweneel (eds) (1996) *Indigenous Revolts in Chiapas and the Andean Highlands* (Amsterdam: CEDLA).

Graham, Richard (1970) 'Brazilian slavery: a review', *Journal of Social History* 3: 431–53.

Graham, Richard (ed.) (1990) *The Idea of Race in Latin America, 1870–1940* (Austin: Texas).

Grieshaber, Erwin P. (1979) 'Hacienda-Indian community relations and Indian acculturation: an historiographical essay', *Latin American Research Review* 14(3): 107–28.

Gros, Christian (1991) *Colombia indígena: identidad cultural y cambio social* (Bogotá: CEREC).

Gros, Christian (1994) 'Noirs, indiennes, créoles en Amérique Latine et aux Antilles', *Cahiers des Amériques Latines* 17: 53–64.

Guss, David (1996) 'Cimarrones, theater, and the state', in Jonathan D. Hill (ed.) *Rethinking History and Myth: Indigenous South American Perspectives on the Past*, pp. 180–92 (Urbana: University of Illinois Press).

Guy, Donna (1991) *Sex and Danger in Buenos Aires: Prostitution, Family, and Nation in Argentina* (Lincoln: University of Nebraska Press).

Hale, Charles (1984) 'Political and social ideas in Latin America', in Leslie Bethell (ed.) *The Cambridge History of Latin America*, vol. 4, pp. 367–442 (Cambridge: Cambridge University Press).

Hale, Charles (1994) *Resistance and Contradiction: Miskitu Indians and the Nicaraguan State, 1894–1987* (Stanford: Stanford University Press).

Hall, Stuart (1980) 'Race, articulation and societies structured in dominance', in UNESCO (ed.) *Sociological Theories: Race and Colonialism*, pp. 305–46 (Paris: UNESCO).

Hall, Stuart (1991) 'The local and the global: globalization and ethnicity', in Anthony King (ed.) *Culture, Globalization and the World-System*, pp. 19–40 (London: Macmillan).

Hall, Stuart (1992a) 'The question of cultural identity', in Stuart Hall, David Held and Tony McGrew (eds) *Modernity and its Futures*, pp. 273–325 (Cambridge: Polity Press).

Hall, Stuart (1992b) 'The West and the Rest: discourse and power', in S. Hall and B. Gieben (eds) *Formations of Modernity*, pp. 275–332 (Milton Keynes: Open University Press).

Hall, Stuart, David Held and Tony McGrew (eds) (1992) *Modernity and its Futures* (Cambridge: Polity Press).

Halperín Donghi, Tulio (1987) 'Economy and society', in Leslie Bethell (ed.) *Spanish America after Independence, c.1820–c.1870*, pp. 1–47 (Cambridge: Cambridge University Press).

Hanchard, Michael (1994) *Orpheus and Power: the Movimento Negro of Rio de Janeiro and São Paulo, Brazil, 1945–1988* (Princeton: Princeton University Press).

Hannerz, Ulf (1980) *Exploring the City: Enquiries toward an Urban Anthropology* (New York: Columbia University Press).

Hanson, Allan (1989) 'The making of the Maori: culture invention and its logic', *American Anthropologist* 91(4): 890–902.

Hanson, Allan (1991) 'Reply to Langdon, Levine and Linnekin', *American Anthropologist* 93(2): 449–50.

Harris, Marvin (1952) 'Race and class in Minas Velhas, a community in the mountain region of Central Brazil', in Charles Wagley (ed.) *Race and Class in Rural Brazil*, pp. 47–81 (Paris: UNESCO).

Harris, Marvin (1970) 'Referential ambiguity in the calculus of Brazilian racial terms', *Southwestern Journal of Anthropology* 27: 1–14.

Harris, Marvin (1974) *Patterns of Race in the Americas* (New York: Norton Library).

Harris, Olivia (1995a) 'The coming of the white people: reflections on the mythologisation of history in Latin America', *Bulletin of Latin American Research* 14(1): 9–24.

Harris, Olivia (1995b) 'Ethnic identity and market relations: Indians and mestizos in the Andes', in Brooke Larson, Olivia Harris and Enrique Tandeter (eds) *Ethnicity, Markets and Migration in the Andes: At the Crossroads of History and Anthropology*, pp. 351–90 (Durham: Duke University Press).

Harvey, David (1989) *The Condition of Postmodernity* (Oxford: Blackwell).

Hasenbalg, Carlos (1979) *Discriminação e desigualdades raciais no Brazil*, translated from the English PhD thesis by Patrick Burglin (Rio de Janeiro: Graal).

Hasenbalg, Carlos (1985) 'Race and socioeconomic inequalities in Brazil', in Pierre-Michel Fontaine (ed.) *Race, Class and Power in Brazil*, pp. 25–41 (Los Angeles: Center for Afro-American Studies, University of California).

Hastrup, Kirsten and Peter Elsass (1990) 'Anthropological advocacy: a contradiction in terms', *Current Anthropology* 31(3): 301–11.

Hechter, Michael (1975) *Internal Colonialism: The Celtic Fringe in British National Development, 1536–1966* (London: Routledge and Kegan Paul).

Helg, Aline (1995) *Our Rightful Share: The Afro-Cuban Struggle for Equality, 1886–1912* (Chapel Hill: University of North Carolina Press).

Hemming, John (1987) 'Indians and the frontier', in Leslie Bethell (ed.) *Colonial Brazil*, pp. 145–89 (Cambridge: Cambridge University Press).

Hendrickson, Carol (1991) 'Images of the Indian in Guatemala: the role of indigenous dress in Indian and ladino constructions', in Greg Urban and Joel Sherzer (eds) *Nation-States and Indians in Latin America*, pp. 286–306 (Austin: University of Texas Press).

Henfrey, Colin (1981) 'The hungry imagination: social formation, popular culture and ideology in Bahia', in Simon Mitchell (ed.) *The Logic of Poverty: The Case of the Brazilian North East*, pp. 58–108 (London: Routledge and Kegan Paul).

Herskovits, Melville (1966) *The New World Negro*, edited by Frances Herskovits (London: Indiana University Press).

Hewitt de Alcántara, Cynthia (1984) *Anthropological Perspectives on Rural Mexico* (London: Routledge and Kegan Paul).

Heuman, Gad (ed.) (1986) *Out of the House of Bondage: Runaways, Resistance and Maronnage in Africa and the New World* (London: Frank Cass).

Hill, Jonathan D. (ed.) (1988) *Rethinking History and Myth: Indigenous South American Perspectives on the Past* (Urbana: University of Illinois Press).

Hill, Jonathan D. (ed.) (1996) *History, Power, and Identity: Ethnogenesis in the Americas, 1492–1992* (Iowa City: University of Iowa Press).

Hobsbawm, Eric and Terence Ranger (eds) (1983) *The Invention of Tradition* (Cambridge: Cambridge University Press).

Hodgen, Margaret (1964) *Early Anthropology in the Sixteenth and Seventeenth Centuries* (Philadelphia: University of Pennsylvannia Press).

Hoetink, Harry (1969) 'Race relations in Curaçao and Surinam', in Laura Foner and Eugene Genovese (eds) *Slavery in the New World: A Reader in Comparative History*, pp. 178–88 (Englewood Cliffs, NJ: Prentice-Hall).

hooks, bell (1981) *Ain't I a Woman? Black Women and Feminism* (London: Pluto Press).

hooks, bell (1991) *Yearning: Race, Gender and Cultural Politics* (London: Turnaround Press).

Horsman, Reginald (1981) *Manifest Destiny: The Origins of American Racial Anglo-Saxonism* (Cambridge: Harvard University Press).

Howe, James (1991) 'An ideological triangle: San Blas Kuna culture, 1915–1925', in Greg Urban and Joel Sherzer (eds) *Nation-States and Indians in Latin America*, pp. 19–52 (Austin: University of Texas Press).

Hugh-Jones, Stephen (1989) 'Wãrĩbi and the white men: history and myth in northwest Amazonia', in Elizabeth Tonkin, Maryon McDonald and Malcolm Chapman (eds) *History and Ethnicity*, pp. 53–70 (London: Routledge).

Hulme, Peter (1986) *Colonial Encounters: Europe and the Native Caribbean, 1492–1797* (London: Methuen).

Hyam, Ronald (1990) *Empire and Sexuality: The British Experience* (Manchester: Manchester Univerity Press).

Ianni, Octavio (1966) *Raças e clases sociais no Brazil* (Rio de Janerio: Civilizacão Brasileira).

Ianni, Octavio (1972) 'Race and class in Latin America', in A.H. Richmond (ed.) *Readings in Race and Ethnic Relations*, pp. 237–56 (Oxford: Pergamon).

Ireland, Rowan (1992) *Kingdom's Come: Religion and Politics in Brazil* (Pittsburgh: University of Pittsburgh Press).

Isbell, Billie Jean (1978) *To Defend Ourselves: Ecology and Ritual in an Andean Village* (Austin: Institute of Latin American Studies, University of Texas).

Jackson, Jean (1991) 'Being and becoming an indian in the Vaupés', in Greg Urban and Joel Sherzer (eds) *Nation-States and Indians in Latin America*, pp. 131–55 (Austin: University of Texas Press).

Jackson, Jean (1995) 'Culture, genuine and spurious: the politics of Indianness in the Vaupés, Colombia', *American Ethnologist* 22(1): 3–27.

Jameson, Fredric (1991) *Postmodernism, or the Cultural Logic of Late Capitalism* (Durham: Duke University Press).

Jaramillo Uribe, Jaime (1968) *Ensayos sobre historia social colombiana.* vol. 1. *La sociedad neogranadina* (Bogotá: Universidad Nacional).

Jaulin, R. (1970) *La paix blanche: introduction à l'étnocide* (Paris: Editions du Seuil).

Jones, E.L. (1981) *The European Miracle: Environments, Economies, and Geopolitics in the History of Europe and Asia* (Cambridge: Cambridge University Press).

Jordan, Winthrop (1969) 'American chiaroscuro: the status and definition of mulattoes in the British colonies', in Laura Foner and Eugene Genovese (eds) *Slavery in the New World: A Reader in Comparative History*, pp. 189–201 (Englewood Cliffs, NJ: Prentice-Hall).

Jordan, Winthrop (1977) *White over Black: American Attitudes towards the Negro, 1550–1812* (New York: Norton).

Kay, Cristobal (1989) *Latin American Theories of Development and Underdevelopment* (London: Routledge).

Kearney, Michael (1996) 'Indigenous ethnicity and mobilization in Latin America', *Latin American Perspectives*, special issue on Ethnicity and Class in Latin America, 23(2): 5–16.

Keith, Michael and Malcolm Cross (1993) 'Racism and the postmodern city', in Michael Keith and Malcolm Cross (eds) *Racism, the City, and the State*, pp. 1–30 (London: Routledge).

Kizca, John (1995) 'Recent books on ethnohistory and ethnic relations in colonial Mexico', *Latin American Research Review* 30(3): 239–53.

Klein, Herbert (1986) *African Slavery in Latin America and the Caribbean* (Oxford: Oxford University Press).

Kloosterman, Jeanette (1996) 'The *cabildo* of the *resguardo* Muellamués (South-Colombia): between disappearance and resurrection', in Ton Salman (ed.) *The Legacy of the Disinherited. Popular Culture in Latin America: Modernity, Globalization, Hybridity and Authenticity*, pp. 113–35 (Amsterdam: CEDLA).

Knight, Alan (1990) 'Racism, revolution and *indigenismo* in Mexico, 1910–1940', in Richard Graham (ed.) *The Idea of Race in Latin America*, pp. 71–113 (Austin: University of Texas Press).

Knowles, C. and S. Mercer (1992) 'Feminism and antiracism:

an exploration of the political possibilities', in J. Donald and A. Rattansi (eds) *'Race', Culture and Difference*, pp. 104–25 (London: Sage).

Kuhn, Thomas (1970) *The Structure of Scientific Revolutions* (Chicago: University of Chicago Press).

Kuper, Leo and M.G. Smith (eds) (1969) *Pluralism in Africa* (Berkeley: University of California Press).

Landry, Donna and Gerald MacLean (1993) *Materialist Feminisms* (Oxford: Blackwell).

Langdon, E. Jean Matteson and Gerhard Baer (eds) (1992) *Portals of Power: Shamanism in South America* (Albuquerque: University of New Mexico Press).

Larson, Brooke, Olivia Harris and Enrique Tandeter (eds) (1995) *Ethnicity, Markets and Migration in the Andes: At the Crossroads of History and Anthropology* (Durham: Duke University Press).

Lewis, Oscar (1951) *Life in a Mexican Village: Tepoztlán Restudied* (Urbana: University of Illinois).

Lieberman, Leonard and Reynolds, Larry T. (eds) (1996) 'Race: the deconstruction of a scientific concept', in L.T. Reynolds and L. Lieberman (eds) *Race and Other Misadventures: Essays in Honor of Ashley Montagu in his Ninetieth Year*, pp. 142–73 (Dix Hills, NY: General Hall Inc.).

Lima, Antonio Carlos de Souza (1991) 'On indigenism and nationality in Brazil', in Greg Urban and Joel Sherzer (eds) *Nation-States and Indians in Latin America*, pp. 236–58 (Austin: University of Texas Press).

Linger, Daniel Touro (1992) *Dangerous Encounters: Meanings of Violence in a Brazilian City* (Stanford: Stanford University Press).

Lockhart, James and Stuart Schwartz (1983) *Early Latin America* (Cambridge: Cambridge University Press).

Lombardi, John V. (1974) 'Comparative slave systems in the Americas: a critical review', in Richard Graham and Peter Smith (eds) *New Approaches to Latin American History*, pp. 156–74 (Austin: University of Texas Press).

Long, Norman (1977) *An Introduction to the Sociology of Rural Development* (London: Tavistock).

Lyons, Andrew (1996) 'The Neotenic career of M.F. Ashley Montagu', in L.T. Reynolds and L. Lieberman (eds) *Race and Other Misadventures: Essays in Honor of Ashley Montagu in his Ninetieth Year*, pp. 3–22 (Dix Hills, NY: General Hall Inc.).

MacDonald, John and Leatrice MacDonald (1978) 'The black

family in the Americas: a review of the literature', *Sage Race Relations Abstracts* 3(1): 1–42.

McCaa, Robert (1984) '*Calidad*, class and marriage in colonial Mexico: the case of Parral, 1780–1790', *Hispanic American Historical Review* 64(3): 477–501.

McClintock, Anne (1993) 'Family feuds: gender, nationalism and the family', *Feminist Review* 44: 61–80.

McGarrity, Gayle and Osvaldo Cárdenas (1995) 'Cuba', in Minority Rights Group (ed.) *No Longer Invisible: Afro-Latin Americans Today*, pp. 77–108 (London: Minority Rights Group).

Mallon, Florencia E. (1992) 'Indian communities, political cultures and the state in Latin America, 1780–1990', *Journal of Latin American Studies*, 24, Quincentenary Supplement: 35–53.

Manuel, Peter (1995) *Caribbean Currents: Caribbean Music from Rumba to Reggae* (Philadelphia: Temple University Press).

Marable, Manning (1995) *Beyond Black and White* (London: Verso).

Marcus, George and Michael Fischer (1986) *Anthropology as Cultural Critique* (Chicago: University of Chicago Press).

Martinez-Alier, Verena (1989 [1974]) *Marriage, Colour and Class in Nineteenth-Century Cuba: A Study of Racial Attitudes and Sexual Values in a Slave Society* (Ann Arbor: University of Michigan Press).

Mason, Peter (1990) *Deconstructing America: Representations of the Other* (London: Routledge).

Mayr, Ernst (1982) *The Growth of Biological Thought: Diversity, Evolution and Inheritance* (Cambridge, Mass.: Harvard University Press).

Meek, Ronald (1976) *Social Science and the Ignoble Savage* (Cambridge: Cambridge University Press).

Merchant, Carol (1983) *The Death of Nature: Women, Ecology and the Scientific Revolution* (San Francisco: Harper and Row).

Mintz, Sidney and Richard Price (1976) *An Anthropological Approach to the Afro-American Past: A Caribbean Perspective* (Philadelphia: Institute for the Study of Human Issues).

Mitchell, J. Clyde (1956) *The Kalela Dance: Aspects of Social Relationships among Urban Africans in Northern Rhodesia* (Manchester: Manchester University Press for the Rhodes-Livingstone Institute).

Mörner, Magnus (1967) *Race Mixture in the History of Latin America* (Boston: Little Brown).

Nash, June (1995) 'The reassertion of indigenous identity: Mayan responses to state intervention in Chiapas', *Latin American Research Review* 30(3): 7–41.

Nash, Manning (1958) *Machine Age Maya: The Industrialization of a Guatemalan Community* (Mensha, Wis.: American Anthropological Association).

Nash, Manning (1970) 'The impact of mid-nineteenth century economic change upon the indians of Middle America', in Magnus Mörner (ed.) *Race and Class in Latin America*, pp. 170–83 (New York: Columbia University Press).

Nogueira, Oracy (1955) 'Preconceito racial de marca e preconceito racial de origem', in *Annais do XXXVI Congreso Internacional de Americanistas*, pp. 409–34 (São Paulo: Editora Anhembí).

Omi, Michael and Howard Winant (1986) *Racial Formation in the USA from the 1960s to the 1980s* (New York: Routledge).

Ortiz, Fernando (1973 [1906]) *Hampa afrocubana: los negros brujos* (Miami: Ediciones Universal).

Ortiz, Fernando (1984) *Ensayos etnográficos*, edited by Miguel Barnet and Angel Fernández (Havana: Editorial de Ciencias Sociales).

Pagden, Anthony (1982) *The Fall of Natural Man: The American Indian and the Origins of Comparative Ethnology* (Cambridge: Cambridge University Press).

Pagden, Anthony (1993) *European Encounters with the New World* (New Haven: Yale University Press).

Paine, Robert (ed.) (1985) *Advocacy and Anthropology* (St Johns: Memorial University of Newfoundland).

Palmié, Stephan (1995) 'Against syncretism: "Africanizing" and "Cubanizing" discourses in North American *òrìsà* worship', in Richard Fardon (ed.) *Counterworks: Managing the Diversity of Knowledge*, pp. 73–104 (London: Routledge).

Parker, A., M. Russo, D. Sommer and P. Yaeger (eds) (1992) *Nationalisms and Sexualities* (London: Routledge).

Pierson, Donald (1942) *Negroes in Brazil: A Study of Race Contact at Bahía* (Chicago: Chicago University Press).

Pieterse, J. Nederveen (1992) *White on Black: Images of Africa and Blacks in Western Popular Culture* (New Haven: Yale University Press).

Pineda Camacho, Roberto (1984) 'La reivindicación del indio en el pensamiento social colombiano, 1850–1950', in Jaime Arocha and Nina de Friedemann (eds) *Un siglo de investigación social la antropología colombiana*, pp. 197–251 (Bogotá: Etno).

Platt, Tristan (1993) 'Simón Bolívar, the sun of justice and the Amerindian virgin – Andean conceptions of the *patria* in nineteenth-century Potosí', *Journal of Latin American Studies* 25(1): 159–85.

Platt, Tristan (1995) 'Ethnic calendars and market interventions among the *ayullus* of Lipes during the nineteenth century', in Brooke Larson, Olivia Harris and Enrique Tandeter (eds) *Ethnicity, Markets, and Migration in the Andes: At the Crossroads of History and Anthropology*, pp. 259–96 (Durham: Duke University Press).

Poole, Deborah and Gerardo Renique (1991) 'The new chroniclers of Peru: US scholars and their "Shining Path" of peasant rebellion', *Bulletin of Latin American Research* 10(2): 133–91.

Prescott, Laurence E. (1985) 'Jorge Artel frente a Nicolás Guillén: dos poetas mulatos ante la poesía negra hispanoamericana', in Raymond L. Williams (ed.) *Ensayos de Literatura Colombiana*, pp. 129–36 (Bogotá: Plaza y Janes).

Price, Richard (1979) 'Introduction' and 'Afterword', in Richard Price (ed.) *Maroon Societies: Rebel Slave Communities in the Americas*, pp. 1–30 and 417–31. 2nd edn (Garden City, NY: Anchor Books).

Price, Richard (1983) *First Time: The Historical Vision of an Afro-American People* (Baltimore: Johns Hopkins University Press).

Radcliffe, Sarah (1990) 'Ethnicity, patriarchy and incorporation into the nation: female migrants as domestic servants in southern Peru', *Environment and Planning D: Society and Space* 8: 379–93.

Rappaport, Joanne (1990) *The Politics of Memory: Native Historical Interpretation in the Colombian Andes* (Cambridge: Cambridge University Press).

Rappaport, Joanne (1994) *Cumbe Reborn: An Andean Ethnography of History* (Chicago: University of Chicago Press).

Redfield, Robert (1930) *Tepoztlán: A Mexican Village* (Chicago: University of Chicago Press).

Redfield, Robert (1956) 'The relations between Indians and ladinos in Agua Escondida, Guatemala', *América Indígena* 16: 253–76.

Reily, Suzel Ana (1994) 'Macunaíma's music: national identity and ethnomusicological research in Brazil', in Martin Stokes (ed.) *Ethnicity, Identity and Music: The Musical Construction of Place*, pp. 71–96 (Oxford: Berg).

Renard, Marie-Christine (1994) 'Le Chiapas est aussi le Mexique: neo-zapatisme et changement politique', *Cahiers des Amériques Latines* 17: 5–23.

Rex, John (1986) 'Class analysis: a Weberian approach', in John

Rex and David Mason (eds) *Theories of Race and Ethnic Relations*, pp. 64–83 (Cambridge: Cambridge University Press).

Reynolds, Larry T. and Leonard Lieberman (eds) (1996) *Race and Other Misadventures: Essays in Honor of Ashley Montagu in his Ninetieth Year* (Dix Hills, NY: General Hall Inc.).

Rivera Cusicanqui, Silvia (1993) 'Anthropology and society in the Ande: themes and issues', *Critique of Anthropology* 13(1): 77–96.

Roberts, Bryan (1974) 'The interrelationships between city and provinces in Peru and Guatemala', Wayne Cornelius and Felicity Trueblood (eds) *Anthropological Perspectives on Latin American Urbanization*, pp. 207–36 (Beverley Hills: Sage).

Roberts, John Storm (1979) *The Latin Tinge: The Impact of Latin American Music on the United States* (New York: Oxford University Press).

Rostas, Susanna and André Droogers (eds) (1993) *The Popular Use of Popular Religion in Latin America* (Amsterdam: CEDLA).

Rout, Leslie (1976) *The African Experience in Spanish America: 1502 to the Present Day* (Cambridge: Cambridge University Press).

Russell-Wood, A.J.R. (1982) *The Black Man in Slavery and Freedom in Colonial Brazil* (London: St Antony's College and Macmillan).

Sahlins, Marshal (1993) 'Goodbye to tristes tropes: ethnography in the context of modern world history', *Journal of Modern History* 65: 1–25.

Said, Edward (1985) *Orientalism: Western Concepts of the Orient* (Harmondsworth: Penguin).

Sanjek, Roger (1971) 'Brazilian racial terms: some aspects of meaning and learning', *American Anthropologist* 73: 1126–44.

Saunders, A.C. de C.M. (1982) *A Social History of Black Slaves and Freedmen in Portugal, 1441–1555* (Cambridge: Cambridge University Press).

Scherrer, Christian P. (1994) 'Regional autonomy in Eastern Nicaragua (1990–1994)', in W.J. Assies and A.J. Hoekema (eds) *Indigenous Peoples' Experiences with Self-Government*, pp. 109–48 (Amsterdam: IWGIA and the University of Amsterdam).

Schryer, Frans J. (1990) *Ethnicity and Class Conflict in Rural Mexico* (Princeton: Princeton University Press).

Schwarz, Roberto (1992) *Misplaced Ideas: Essays on Brazilian Culture*, edited and with an introduction by John Gledson (London: Verso).

Seed, Patricia (1982) 'Social dimensions of race: Mexico City,

1753', *Hispanic American Historical Review* 62(4): 569–606.

Silva, Nelson do Valle (1985) 'Updating the cost of not being white in Brazil', in Pierre-Michel Fontaine (ed.) *Race, Class and Power in Brazil*, pp. 42–55 (Los Angeles: Center for Afro-American Studies, University of Califonia).

Skidmore, Thomas (1972) 'Towards a comparative analysis of race relations since abolition in Brazil and the United States', *Journal of Latin American Studies* 4(1): 1–28.

Skidmore, Thomas (1974) *Black into White: Race and Nationality in Brazilian Thought* (New York: Oxford University Press).

Skidmore, Thomas (1993) 'Bi-racial USA vs. multi-racial Brazil: is the contrast still valid?', *Journal of Latin American Studies* 25: 373–86.

Smedley, Audrey (1993) *Race in North America: Origin and Evolution of a World View* (Oxford: Westview).

Smith, Carol A. (ed.) (1990) *Guatemalan Indians and the State, 1540–1988* (Austin: University of Texas Press).

Smith, M.G. (1965) *The Plural Society in the British West Indies* (Berkeley: University of California Press).

Solaún, Mauricio and Sidney Kronus (1973) *Discrimination Without Violence: Miscegenation and Racial Conflict in Latin America* (New York: John Wiley and Sons).

Solomos, John (1986) 'Varieties of Marxist conceptions of "race", class and the state: a critical analysis', in John Rex and David Mason (eds) *Theories of Race and Ethnic Relations*, pp. 84–109 (Cambridge: Cambridge University Press).

Solomos, John (1989) *Race and Racism in Contemporary Britain* (London: Routledge).

Stavenhagen, Rodolfo (1975) *Social Classes in Agrarian Societies* (Garden City, NY: Anchor Books).

Stavenhagen, Rodolfo (1996) *Ethnic Conflicts and the Nation-State* (Houndsmills: Macmillan; New York: St Martins Press).

Stepan, Nancy (1982) *The Idea of Race in Science: Great Britain, 1800–1950* (London: Macmillan).

Stepan, Nancy (1991) *'The Hour of Eugenics': Race, Gender and Nation in Latin America* (Ithaca: Cornell University Press).

Stern, Steve J. (ed.) (1987) *Resistance, Rebellion and Consciousness in the Andean Peasant World, 18th to 20th Centuries* (Madison: University of Wisconsin Press).

Stocking, George (1982) *Race, Culture and Evolution: Essays on the History of Anthropology* (2nd edn Chicago: Chicago University Press).

Stone, John (1979) 'Introduction: internal colonialism in comparative perspective', *Ethnic and Racial Studies* 2(3): 253–9.

Stutzman, Ronald (1981) '*El mestizaje*: an all-inclusive ideology of exclusion', in Norman E. Whitten (ed.) *Cultural Transformations and Ethnicity in Modern Ecuador*, pp. 45–94 (Urbana: University of Illinois Press).

Tannenbaum, Frank (1948) *Slave and Citizen: The Negro in the Americas* (New York: Vintage Books).

Taussig, Michael (1980) *The Devil and Commodity Fetishism in South America* (Chapel Hill: University of North Carolina Press).

Taussig, Michael (1987) *Shamanism, Colonialism and the Wild Man: A Study in Terror and Healing* (Chicago: Chicago University Press).

Tax, Sol (1942) 'Ethnic relations in Guatemala', *América Indígena*, 2(4): 43–8.

Tax, Sol (1953) *Penny Capitalism: A Guatemalan Indian Economy* (Washington: Smithsonian Institution).

Tax, Sol and Robert Hinshaw (1970) 'Panajachel a generation later', in Walter Goldschmidt and Harry Hoijer (eds) *The Social Anthropology of Latin America: Essays in Honor of Ralph Leon Beals*, pp. 175–98 (Los Angeles: Latin American Center, University of California).

Toplin, Robert (1981) *Freedom and Prejudice: The Legacy of Slavery in the USA and Brazil* (Westport: Greenwood Press).

Toplin, Robert B. (1971) 'Reinterpreting comparative race relations: the United States and Brazil', *Journal of Black Studies*, 2(2): 135–56.

Treece, David (1990) 'Indigenous peoples in the Brazilian Amazon and the expansion of the economic frontier', in David Goodman and Anthony Hall (eds) *The Future of Amazonia: Destruction or Sustainable Development?*, pp. 264–87 (London: Macmillan).

Tumin, Melvin (1952) *Caste in a Peasant Society* (Princeton: Princeton University Press).

Turner, Bryan (ed.) (1990) *Theories of Modernity and Postmodernity* (London: Sage).

Turner, Terence (1991) 'Representing, resisting, rethinking: historical transformations of Kayapo culture and anthropological consciousness', in George Stocking (ed.) *Colonial Situations: Essays on the Contextualization of Ethnographic Knowledge*, pp. 285–313 (Madison: University of Wisconsin Press).

Turner, Terence (1992) 'Defiant images: the Kayapo appropriation of video', *Anthropology Today* 8(6): 5–16.

Urban, Greg and Joel Sherzer (eds) (1991a) *Nation-States and*

Indians in Latin America (Austin: University of Texas Press).

Urban, Greg and Joel Sherzer (1991b) 'Introduction: Indians, nation-states, and culture', in Greg Urban and Joel Sherzer (eds) *Nation-States and Indians in Latin America*, pp. 1–18 (Austin: University of Texas Press).

van den Berghe, Pierre (1967) *Race and Racism* (New York: John Wiley and Sons).

van den Berghe, Pierre (1974a) 'Ethnic terms in Peruvian social science literature', in Pierre van den Berghe (ed.) *Class and Ethnicity in Peru*, pp. 12–22 (Leiden: E.J. Brill).

van den Berghe, Pierre (1974b) 'Introduction', in Pierre van den Berghe (ed.) *Class and Ethnicity in Peru*, pp. 1–11 (Leiden: E.J. Brill).

van den Berghe, Pierre (1975) 'Ethnicity and class in highland Peru', in Leo Despres (ed.) *Ethnicity and Resource Competition in Plural Societies*, pp. 71–85 (The Hague: Mouton).

Varese, Stefano (1996) 'The ethnopolitics of Indian resistance in Latin America', *Latin American Perspectives* 23(2): 58–71.

Vilas, Carlos M. (1989) *State, Class and Ethnicity in Nicaragua* (Boulder: Lynne Rienner).

Wade, Peter (1986) 'Patterns of race in Colombia', *Bulletin of Latin American Research* 5(2): 1–19.

Wade, Peter (1993a) *Blackness and Race Mixture: The Dynamics of Racial Identity in Colombia* (Baltimore: Johns Hopkins University Press).

Wade, P. (1993b) '"Race", Nature and Culture', *Man* 28(1): 1–18.

Wade, Peter (1995a) 'The cultural politics of blackness in Colombia', *American Ethnologist* 22(2): 342–58.

Wade, Peter (1995b) 'Black music and cultural syncretism in Colombia', in Darién J. Davis (ed.) *Slavery and Beyond: The African Impact on Latin America and the Caribbean*, pp. 121–46 (Wilmington, DE: Scholarly Resources Books).

Wade, Peter (n.d.) 'Music, blackness and national identity: three moments in Colombian history'. *Popular Music*, in press.

Wagley, Charles (ed.) (1952) *Race and Class in Rural Brazil* (Paris: UNESCO).

Watanabe, John (1995) 'Unimagining the Maya: anthropologists, others and the inescapable hubris of authorship', *Bulletin of Latin American Research* 14(1): 25–46.

Weiner, Michael (1995) 'Discourses of race, nation and empire in pre-1945 Japan', *Ethnic and Racial Studies*, 18(3): 433–56.

Wetherell, Margaret and Jonathan Potter (1992) *Mapping the*

Language of Racism: Discourse and the Legitimation of Exploitation (London: Harvester Wheatsheaf).

Whitten, Norman (1965) *Class, Kinship and Power in an Ecuadorian Town* (Stanford: Stanford University Press).

Whitten, Norman (1975) 'Jungle Quechua ethnicity: an Ecuadorian case study', in Leo Despres (ed.) *Ethnicity and Resource Competition in Plural Societies*, pp. 41–69 (The Hague: Mouton).

Whitten, Norman (1976) *Sacha Runa: Ethnicity and Adaptation of Ecuadorian Jungle Quichua* (Urbana: University of Illinois Press).

Whitten, Norman (ed.) (1981a) *Cultural Transformations and Ethnicity in Modern Ecuador* (Urbana: University of Illinois Press).

Whitten, Norman (1981b) 'Introduction', in Norman E. Whitten (ed.) *Cultural Transformations and Ethnicity in Modern Ecuador*, pp. 1–44 (Urbana: University of Illinois Press).

Whitten, Norman (1985) *Sicuanga Runa: The Other Side of Development in Amazonian Ecuador* (Urbana: University of Illinois Press).

Whitten, Norman (1986 [1974]) *Black Frontiersmen: A South American Case*, (2nd edn Prospect Heights, Illinois: Waveland Press).

Whitten, Norman and Nina de Friedemann (1974) 'La cultura negra del litoral ecuatoriano y colombiano: un modelo de adaptación étnica', *Revista Colombiana de Antropología* 17: 75–115.

Whitten, Norman and John Szwed (1970) 'Introduction', in Norman Whitten and John Szwed (eds) *Afro-American Anthropology: Contemporary Perspectives*, pp. 23–53 (New York: Free Press).

Whitten, Norman and Arlene Torres (1992) 'Blackness in the Americas', *NACLA Report on the Americas* 15(4): 16–22.

Williams, Brackette (1989) 'A class act: anthropology and the race to nation across ethnic terrain', *Annual Review of Anthropology* 18: 401–44.

Williams, Brackette (1991) *Stains on my Name, War in my Veins: Guyana and the Politics of Cultural Struggle* (Durham: Duke University Press).

Williams, Raymond (1988) *Keywords* (London: Fontana).

Wilson, Richard (1995a) *Maya Resurgence in Guatemala: Q'echi' Experiences* (Norman: University of Oklahoma Press).

Wilson, Richard (1995b) 'Shifting frontiers: historical transformations of identities in Latin America', *Bulletin of Latin American Research* 14(1): 1–8.

Bibliography

Winant, Howard (1992) 'Rethinking race in Brazil', *Journal of Latin American Studies* 24: 173–92.

Winant, Howard (1993) 'Difference and inequality: postmodern racial politics in the United States', in M. Cross and M. Keith (eds) *Racism, the City and the State*, pp. 108–27 (London: Routledge).

Wolf, Eric (1955) 'Types of Latin American peasantry: a preliminary discussion', *American Anthropologist* 57: 452–71.

Wolpe, Harold (1975) 'The theory of internal colonialism: the South African case'. In I. Oxaal, T. Barnett and D. Booth (eds) *Beyond the Sociology of Development*, pp. 229–52 (London: Routledge and Kegan Paul).

Wright, Winthrop (1990) *Café con Leche: Race, Class and National Image in Venezuela* (Austin: University of Texas Press).

Young, Robert (1995) *Colonial Desire: Hybridity in Theory, Culture and Race* (London: Routledge).

Yuval-Davis, Nira and Floya Anthias (eds) (1989) *Woman-Nation-State* (London: Macmillan).

Zamosc, Leon (1994) 'Agrarian protest and the Indian movement in the Ecuadorian highlands', *Latin American Research Review* 29(3): 37–68.

Zanotta Machado, Lia (1994) 'Indigenous communitarianism as a critique of modernity and its juridical implications', in W.J. Assies and A.J. Hoekema (eds) *Indigenous Peoples' Experiences with Self-Government*, pp. 73–91 (Amsterdam: IWGIA and the University of Amsterdam).

INDEX

Note: Authors are indexed if quoted in the text, but not if only cited

Index

race in, 56–7, 68, 71; black culture in, 76; black political mobilisation, 97; class and race in, 53–7; gender inequality in, 102; ideology of *indigenismo*, 32, 33; Kayapo indians, 99–100, 114, 118; mixedness in, 34, 49–50, 51, 83; place of blacks in, 33, 53; place of mulattoes in, 50, 69, 70, 71–3; racial categories in, 29–30, 72; slavery in, 27, 49; status of indians in, 28; studies of racism in, 68–73; UNESCO studies, 51–3, 112, *see also* Amazonia; Bahía

Cancian, Francesca and Frank, 42
candomblé religious practices, Bahía, 78, 93, 100
capitalism, 71, 82–3, 112
Cardoso, Fernando Henrique, 68–9
Caribbean, cultural influence, 93–4, 98
Casas, Bartolomé de las, 27
castas (castes), 29
caste, US usage of, 52, 53
Catholic Church, 91, 98; in Brazil, 100, 101; influence on integration, 50, 74
Chiapas, Mexico: Havard Project, 42; interethnic relations in, 44–7, 62; liberation theology in, 101; Zapatista movement, 98, 105
China, race in, 121n
cholo, intermediate category in Peru, 38, 41, 61–2, 63–4
Christendom, exclusivism of, 8–9
Christian Base Communities, 95, 101
Christianity, in Africa, 26

Chuschi, Peru, ethnic boundaries in, 66–7
Cimmarón organisation, 98
class: and black organisations, 97–8, 99; and cultural difference, 17–18; and indigenous identity, 98–9; and interethnic relations, 44–6, 99; in Mexico, 41; reductionism, 70; relationship to race, 22–4, 53–5
Cohen, Abner, 17, 60
Colby, Ben, 44–5
Colombia, 21, 35, 89, 91–2; attribution of magical powers, 92–3; black organisations, 95, 97–8, 104; official multiculturalism, 106–7; racial categories in, 29, 37; status of blacks in, 35–7, 49, 85, 113; status of mixedness, 32, 85–6; studies of black culture in, 75–6, 93–4, 117
colonialism, 30–1; analysis of, 47–8, 79; and gender, 102–3; internal, 64–6, 85; and sexuality, 103; slavery under, 26–8; and utilitarianism, 11–12
communities: closed, 42–3, 66; imagined, 83–4; open, 41–2, *see also* regions of refuge
conquistadors, 26–7
creoles (*criollos*), 28
Cuba, 29, 31, 49, 102; *afro-cubanismo* in, 33
cultural difference, 7; and class, 17–18; ethnicity as, 16–17, 37; and place, 18–19
cultural ecology, growth of, 40–1
culture, 33, 63, 82; and accommodation, 86–7; acculturation, 43, 47; and class identification, 46; constructed, 91–2; and economics, 112; and ethnic identity, 90, 92
Cuvier, Georges, 10

147